HOLINESS.COM

DATING SURVIVAL GUIDE

By

Shawn David Jackson
(Just A Brother)

First Edition
[*Author's Deluxe Version*]

Holiness.com, International

HOLINESS.COM
DATING SURVIVAL GUIDE
by Shawn David Jackson

Published by:
Holiness.com, International
PMB 165
1271 Washington Ave.
San Leandro, CA 94577
orders@Holiness.com
http://www.Holiness.com

Unless otherwise stated, all Scripture quotations are taken from the *Authorized King James Version* of the Bible.

Scripture quotations marked *(TLB)* are taken from *The Living Bible*, copyright ©1971. Used by permission of Tyndale House Publishers, Inc., Wheaton, IL 60189 USA. All rights reserved.

Publisher's Cataloging-in-Publication Data
Jackson, Shawn.

Holiness.com dating survival guide / by Shawn David Jackson. -- 1st ed. -- San Leandro, CA : Holiness.com International, 2003.

p. ; cm.

ISBN: 0-9743831-8-X

1. Dating (Social customs)--Religious aspects.
2. Man-woman relationships--Religious aspects.
3. Christian life. I. Title. II. Dating survival guide. III. Holiness.com.

HQ801 .A3 J33 2003

306.73--dc22   3012
Library of Congress Control Number: 2003114727

CONTENTS

Contents

PREFACE

Yesterday, as my cousins and I sat around a table in a popular Berkeley, California restaurant overlooking the San Francisco Bay, the fact that I had written a book on dating popped into our discussion. One of my cousins seemed quite surprised that I had written a book about dating. With amazement in his eyes, and sarcasm in his voice, he questioned whether I had enough "experience" at dating to write a book.

It seems to me, that underlying my cousin's question is the false belief that a man must live the life of a "playboy" in order to gain the wisdom necessary to advise others on <u>appropriate</u> dating guidelines.

Let me be perfectly honest with you: this book is not a guide on how to seduce women (or men) into satisfying one's sinful desires at some sleazy, flea-bitten roadside motel.

If you haven't guessed it yet:
"Yes, I am a Christian, and proud to be one."

Many years ago I asked Jesus Christ to forgive me of all the sins I was involved in, or had practiced in the past. I asked Jesus Christ to be the Lord of my life and to help me live according to God's standard, which the Holy Bible declares.

When Christ is Lord of a person's life, he or she will exhibit godly behavior in every facet of life, even while navigating the dating scene. Thus, you will find each chapter in this guide written from the perspective of someone who holds that even a person's dating behavior should conform to the standards of Biblical Christian behavior.

Why did I write this book?

I wrote this book because I love you, and I want to stop the needless emotional pain and physical and spiritual danger that people often subject themselves to by engaging in horrible dating practices.

ACKNOWLEDGEMENTS

It is with sincere gratitude that I acknowledge some of my family and friends for their place in my life and in my heart, and their contribution to what I have accomplished in writing this book:

To my Wife, who maintained a genuine interest in the progress of the book and endured the long hours I spent while the Holy fire burned within me to complete this work.

To my Children, who brought me cookies and milk and demonstrated a willingness to help any way they could, as I banged away at the computer keyboard.

To my Mom, Dad, Grandparents, and Great Grandparents, who encouraged within me a love of God's holy word (the Bible) from my infancy.

To the Ferguson family, who were instrumental by divine providence in my meeting and dating my future wife, while I was still single and in search of God's choice for a lifelong companion.

To all of my manuscript reviewers, whose help and suggestions have been invaluable.

To Pastor Leon Jackson, who has been a true counselor and advisor during the development and publication of this work.

To Eric Polak, the masterful artist who took my scratchy design notes and created the beautiful scene on the front cover.

To all my kin, friends, and business associates, without whose help this book would not be the success that it is.

* * * * * * * * * * * * * * *

EIGHT TRUTHS

As you read this dating guide, please keep the following eight truths in mind:

> 1) There are people who go to church (who may even be card-carrying members of a particular church fellowship) who are not necessarily Christians.

> 2) Christians are NOT to date non-Christians – see the Holiness.com Fireside Chat discussion on this same topic. (For your convenience, I have included this article in an attachment of this book.)

> 3) It is totally possible for someone who is truly a Christian to give advice that is contrary to Biblical values. This bad advice will lead the follower of the advice in a direction that is opposite to God's divine plan for the individual.

> Matthew 16:21-23 says: "From that time forth began Jesus to shew unto his disciples, how that he must go unto Jerusalem, and suffer many things of the elders and chief priests and

scribes, and be killed, and be raised again the third day. Then Peter took him, and began to rebuke him, saying, Be it far from thee, Lord: this shall not be unto thee. But he turned, and said unto Peter, Get thee behind me, Satan: thou art an offence unto me: for thou savourest not the things that be of God, but those that be of men." Peter, indeed was a follower of Christ (see Matthew 16:16-19); however, Peter in trying to convince Christ not to suffer for humanity, was really putting forward the path that Satan wanted Jesus to follow. Look at the motive as to why someone is trying to get you to do something (what self-interest do they have to gain if you do what they ask?). And, look at the scriptural basis of what a person is telling you.

4) Regardless of what you were before you accepted Christ, the Biblical-Christian standard for living is <u>Holiness</u>. In the past, you may have been a "swinger", "player", or whatever other name you went by, but as a Christian, God is calling you to honesty and purity.

5) A Christian must understand that certain sins do possess a level of pleasure, and this tends to make these sins all the more alluring and dangerous. Observe how Proverbs 9:16-18 exposes the wicked words of the seductress who lures fools into her home – the seductress says "Whoso is simple, let him turn in hither: and as for him that wanteth understanding, she saith to him, Stolen waters are sweet, and bread eaten in secret is pleasant. But he knoweth not that the dead are there; and that her guests are in the depths of hell."

6) Do not think that your bloodline, or your political connections, or your money, or your education places you on a pinnacle above all other Christians: "...have no confidence in the flesh." (Philippians 3:3). But, all of us Christians were saved from sin by the work of Christ, and as we tread the

path of Holiness, we must "Watch and pray, that ye enter not into temptation: the spirit indeed is willing, but the flesh is weak." (Matthew 26:41)

7) If, as you read the following material, you find that you have not been following wisdom in certain areas of your life, many of you will be tempted to let your pride cause you to defend some past mistake. I caution you that when you become aware of a better way, it is best to just pick up from where you are now and begin to follow the better way.

8) A person can be gifted by God with some great and notable talent; this does not make them the ideal choice for a marriage partner. For example: a man can have the greatest musical gift as far as singing and playing an instrument, and yet be selfish and immature when it comes to interpersonal relationships. It amazes me how men and women swoon (become dizzy with love) in the presence of gifted church celebrity types. Some men and women will pursue serious relationships (even marriage) with people based solely upon how that celebrity person makes them feel while displaying the gift or talent.

* * * * * * * * * * * * * * *

WHY A DATING SURVIVAL GUIDE

Some of you are possibly questioning why Holiness.com has chosen to set forth instructions with regard to dating; maybe you think that unmarried Christians don't have a need for any additional instructions on the subject. Or, possibly you believe that everything is going just fine in the Christian dating scene. Well, let me begin by sharing two true stories, of which I have direct information:

Years ago, there was a young lady of the church whom a certain young man would take to social events. This young lady did not live with her parents, but had her own apartment. So, when the young man would arrive at this attractive young lady's apartment to take her on their date, He would wait outside the apartment to allow her to finish getting ready for their date, and would meet her outside when she was ready to leave for their date. Apparently, the young lady could not understand why the young man made a practice of not waiting inside her apartment. And, as I understood by way of hearsay report, her mother thought it was a ridiculous habit of the young man not to wait inside her daughter's apartment.

You see, it was not that the young man felt he was too good to enter his female friend's apartment; quite the contrary. Knowing that this person was indeed attractive, knowing that so many have fallen into sin visiting their date while alone in an apartment, and knowing that even as a Christian he must avoid placing himself in situations that would cause unnecessary temptation to his flesh, he chose to wait outside the apartment for the young lady. Let me interject the comment that, even if sin would not arise from the young man waiting in the apartment, Christians can cause an appearance of something that looks scandalous by not using caution.

The relationship between the young man and the young lady eventually dissolved due to circumstances that involved extreme dishonesty. (I won't bore you with the details.) In any case, the young lady continued in her belief of entertaining young gentlemen alone in her apartment. Needless to say, a child was conceived out of wedlock as a result of her entertaining "Christian" men alone in her apartment.

In the second true story I will relate to you, another young attractive lady (different from the lady of the first story) was attending a Christian convention being held in a hotel complex. During the convention, a young man was supposed to have a date with the young lady. The young lady was sharing a hotel room with an older Christian woman. When the young man called the young lady at her hotel room, she informed him that she was still getting dressed, and the older Christian she was sharing the room with had already left the room. The young man informed the young lady that he would not come to the room and wait (as she finished dressing), but that he would wait downstairs in the hotel lobby. One of the older Christian ladies with whom the young man was acquainted, heard that he would not go up to the hotel room to wait, and told the young man emphatically that there was nothing wrong with waiting in the room for the young lady.

As I sit here at my desk and recount this story, I literally shake my head in frustration; it is bad enough that many young people don't truly understand the power of their hormones and temptation, but I am perplexed at how older people, who have been married for years and raised children to adulthood, could be so unenlightened as to the danger of Christians of the opposite sex hanging out together (alone) in a hotel room. Some of you are probably nervously laughing right now, because you know how scandalous it sounds to say "a Christian brother is in the hotel room with his date while she finishes dressing". One more thing: the young man and young lady of this story did later go their separate ways. The young lady did continue to pursue a more "progressive" dating style with different men and later did conceive a child outside of marriage.

I need to depart from our main discussion for a moment to deal with an important issue:

> Let me make it perfectly clear that these children who were conceived outside of wedlock in the stories recounted above are totally innocent of any wrongdoing. It is the father and mother who have disobeyed God's command that sex should only be between a man and a woman who are married to each other. And, the solution is not to kill the unborn baby because the child was conceived in less than desirable circumstances.

> Killing the baby that resulted from the fornication of two individuals makes as much sense as King David killing Uriah in an attempt to cover/justify David's adultery with Bathsheba, Uriah's wife. Uriah was a totally innocent party in a situation that occurred because of David's lust. The killing of Uriah (as with the killing of a baby) only compounds the sin of those who have illicit sexual relations. (II Samuel 11:14-15)

Further, conception of a child out of wedlock does not mean two people should necessarily marry; conception does not miraculously turn a bad relationship into a good one, necessarily. Both the father and mother of the child should bear their financial and emotional responsibility without moaning, groaning and complaining.

Finally, if the mother and father receive help from friends and relatives in raising the child, then the mother and father should show great humility and appreciation by treating that help as a gift, not as something the world owes them. Now, back to our main theme.

Some of you may feel that you don't need to follow any instructions or rules regarding dating; you feel that you are totally devil-proof – you feel that you are Superman or Superwoman, and that not even kryptonite can make you weak. [NOTE: in America, Superman is a fictitious cartoon character who is invincible, except when exposed to an element known as kryptonite.] Some people may take Philippians 4:13 as an indication that they can do anything they want, they can say anything they want, they can go anywhere they want; Philippians 4:13 reads: "I can do all things through Christ which strengtheneth me." What this verse is really saying is that Christ strengthens (or gives the power) necessary to enable Christians to achieve all things that are **_within_** God's divine will for a particular person, despite what personal adversities we might face (see verse 12 of the same chapter).

If you are not convinced of the need to have guidelines regarding dating, I ask you to look at the devastation that has resulted from the lack of guidelines. This devastation is quite apparent to me not only in secular/non-Christian society, but within the "progressive" churches of "progressive" cultures. You might think "devastation" is overstating things, but I ask you to look at the number of children conceived by unmarried believers – children who, thus born to unmarried parents, are more likely to be raised in poverty without the blessing and support of a mother and father present in the home. I sincerely believe that many of these single men and women truly accepted Christ, but fell into sin as a result of not following certain dating rules. But, the devastation does not stop at the difficulties caused by singles starting families.

Many singles fall into the sin of fornication and don't conceive children, yet there is still great emotional and spiritual hurt that occurs by giving oneself to another in an intimate way outside of marriage. If you give yourself in an intimate way to your date, when your date gets tired of you and dumps you for his or her next thrill, someone is bound to be deeply emotionally hurt.

Despite the pleasure of fornication, the guilt of sin is present in the heart and mind of those who take part in sexual sins; those who feel no guilt, who have no conscience, are even more pitiable. And, do I need to mention the physical diseases and illnesses among church folk that is the result of promiscuity? I must also ask the question as to why the divorce rate in the church rivals that of the non-believing community: is this not at least partly due to improper dating practices that result in awful marriage choices?

Okay, so hopefully I have convinced you that there is a need for instruction or guidelines regarding dating. Let me say that there is much in the following guidelines that addresses ways to maintain sexual purity. Additionally, there are some things in the following guidelines that address other concepts that are not as much related to sexual purity, but are nevertheless important to dating. Some of these guidelines will help one stay clear of unnecessary temptations to sin; some of these guidelines have more to do with helping individuals avoid unnecessary hardship and pain, and some of these guidelines will simply help prevent you from wasting your time (e.g., with undesirable dating prospects).

I cannot guarantee that these guidelines will always be easy to follow, nor can I guarantee that a person will avoid every possible hardship by following these guidelines. But, I hope these instructions will assist in avoiding obvious and unnecessary trials.

These guidelines are useful for both men and women, and both older and younger singles; they are not the result of some religious person trying to invent some totally new deep and mysterious theories. These guidelines have come about by the study, prayer, and experience of godly people striving to live according to the Bible and the Holiness lifestyle commanded therein.

* * * * * * * * * * * * * * *

LET US BEGIN

I want to first define what I mean by "dating" which, Biblically speaking, only occurs in the context of male-female relationships. The word "dating" or "date" is somewhat challenging to define in a brief sentence or two. But, I feel it is important to attempt a brief definition in order to provide context for the guidelines of this instructional book. So, I provide a definition below that may differ somewhat from the explanation in your dictionary. However, this definition will hopefully be broad enough to include what most people think of when they hear the words "dating" and a "date" in the context of male-and-female relationships.

DATING DEFINED

DATE: When two people of the opposite gender (male and female) and who are not related (not of the same family) mutually agree to attend some event together or visit some particular location together on a social basis, often as the result of the attraction of at least one of the persons to the other.

The word "date" can also be used to refer to either of the persons who attends the event (the "date" as described above).

DATING: Dating can simply be defined as the occurrence of, or participation in one or more dates.

Let me provide an example of what is normally not considered a "date": agreeing to see your dentist to have a tooth pulled would not usually constitute a "date" in our sense of the word, as the meeting is not for recreational reasons (or for the enjoyment of the individuals involved), but for the correction of a medical or health problem.

HOMOSEXUALITY

The subject of homosexuality is being raised more and more in discussions within the religious world. So, I feel compelled to touch on the subject. It has always been contrary to God's plan for two women, or two men (or three men, or four, etc), to try and carry on a romantic relationship. God's standard is that godly romance is authorized only between one man and one woman.

I want to provide you with some of the scriptures in the first chapter of the book of Romans that certify what I am saying regarding homosexuality. I provide Romans 1:18-32 below. Some of these scriptures deal not only with homosexuality, but other heinous acts such as idolatry. I give you this entire passage so that you can see that I have not picked a piece of scripture out of context, but that homosexuality is repulsive to God. Thus Christians should never, ever support homosexuality, but should encourage homosexuals to forsake all of their sins and come to God. Read the scriptures below for yourself in the King James Version (KJV) and The Living Bible (TLB) provided afterward:

18 For the wrath of God is revealed from heaven against

all ungodliness and unrighteousness of men, who hold the truth in unrighteousness;

19 Because that which may be known of God is manifest in them; for God hath shewed it unto them.

20 For the invisible things of him from the creation of the world are clearly seen, being understood by the things that are made, even his eternal power and Godhead; so that they are without excuse:

21 Because that, when they knew God, they glorified him not as God, neither were thankful; but became vain in their imaginations, and their foolish heart was darkened.

22 Professing themselves to be wise, they became fools,

23 And changed the glory of the uncorruptible God into an image made like to corruptible man, and to birds, and fourfooted beasts, and creeping things.

24 Wherefore God also gave them up to uncleanness through the lusts of their own hearts, to dishonor their own bodies between themselves:

25 Who changed the truth of God into a lie, and worshiped and served the creature more than the Creator, who is blessed for ever. Amen.

26 For this cause God gave them up unto vile affections: for even their women did change the natural use into that which is against nature:

27 And likewise also the men, leaving the natural use of the woman, burned in their lust one toward another; men

with men working that which is unseemly, and receiving in themselves that recompense of their error which was meet.

28 And even as they did not like to retain God in their knowledge, God gave them over to a reprobate mind, to do those things which are not convenient;

29 Being filled with all unrighteousness, fornication, wickedness, covetousness, maliciousness; full of envy, murder, debate, deceit, malignity; whisperers,

30 Backbiters, haters of God, despiteful, proud, boasters, inventors of evil things, disobedient to parents,

31 Without understanding, covenantbreakers, without natural affection, implacable, unmerciful:

32 Who knowing the judgment of God, that they which commit such things are worthy of death, not only do the same, but have pleasure in them that do them.

Now the same passage (Romans 1: 18-32) in The Living Bible (TLB) reads as follows:

18 But God shows his anger from heaven against all sinful, evil men who push away the truth from them.

19 For the truth about God is known to them instinctively; God has put this knowledge in their hearts.

20 Since earliest times men have seen the earth and sky and all God made, and have known of his existence and great eternal power. So they will have no excuse [when they stand before God at Judgment Day].

21 Yes, they knew about him all right, but they wouldn't admit it or worship him or even thank him for all his daily care. And after awhile they began to think up silly ideas of what God was like and what he wanted them to do. The result was that their foolish minds became dark and confused.

22 Claiming themselves to be wise without God, they became utter fools instead.

23 And then, instead of worshipping the glorious, ever-living God, they took wood and stone and made idols for themselves, carving them to look like mere birds and animals and snakes and puny men.

24 So God let them go ahead into every sort of sex sin, and do whatever they wanted to – yes, vile and sinful things with each other's bodies.

25 Instead of believing what they knew was the truth about God, they deliberately chose to believe lies. So they prayed to the things God made, but wouldn't obey the blessed God who made these things.

26 That is why God let go of them and let them do all these evil things, so that even their women turned against God's natural plan for them and indulged in sex sin with each other.

27 And the men, instead of having normal sex relationships with women, burned with lust for each other, men doing shameful things with other men and, as a result, getting paid within their own souls with the penalty they so richly deserved.

28 So it was that when thy gave God up and would not even acknowledge him, God gave them up to doing everything their evil minds could think of.

29 Their lives became full of every kind of wickedness and sin, of greed and hate, envy, murder, fighting, lying, bitterness, and gossip.

30 They were backbiters, haters of God, insolent, proud braggarts, always thinking of new ways of sinning and continually being disobedient to their parents.

31 They tried to misunderstand, broke their promises, and were heartless – without pity.

32 They were fully aware of God's death penalty for these crimes, yet they went right ahead and did them anyway, and encouraged others to do them, too.

Take special note of verse 32. If you even encourage or condone homosexual practices, God considers you to be a wicked person. This point must be made because we have some who do not practice homosexuality, but they support homosexual activity, even taking pleasure in promoting homosexual activity as acceptable.

Can a homosexual become a Christian?

If a man or woman forsakes all sin (including homosexuality) and accepts Christ as the Lord (i.e., boss) of his or her life, that man or woman is a Christian. I do recommend that the Christian who has come out of the sin of homosexuality attend a church that will be careful to help that Christian avoid falling back into the bondage of homosexuality.

* * * * * * * * * * * * * * *

WHO SHOULD DATE?

The people who should date are single, unmarried individuals who are eligible/free to marry if they so desire to date. Why do I give such a complicated answer? Well, you have some church folk who have divorced each other because they simply feel they don't like one another any longer – these individuals are not free to date or otherwise develop a romantic relationship with anyone other than that spouse whom they have divorced; I Corinthians 7:10-11 says "And unto the married I command, yet not I, but the Lord, Let not the wife depart from her husband: But and if she depart, let her remain unmarried, or be reconciled to her husband: and let not the husband put away his wife." I think very relevant to this passage in I Corinthians is Matthew 5:32, which states: "But I say unto you, That whosoever shall put away his wife, saving for the cause of fornication, causeth her to commit adultery: and whosoever shall marry her that is divorced committeth adultery."

A case was recently brought to my attention of a well-known missionary who divorced one preacher and now has just married another preacher. My question to the person who approached me with this situation was: "Was the first husband guilty of fornication (i.e. sexual unfaithfulness)?" If the first husband was not guilty of fornication, the missionary and the second preacher are living in <u>adultery</u>. Understand, I am not speaking here to someone who has led a ragged life in their sins and maybe has married a dozen times – when this person comes to Christ, he or she may need a very experienced Pastor to help him or her decipher which, if any, of the 12 marriages is the legitimate one. However, the case I raised concerning the missionary and the two preachers reflects what is happening more and more among so-called "Christians": Church-going individuals who marry within the body of Christ, divorce their spouse, and then re-marry someone else within the body of Christ, and then expect the church to acknowledge this second marriage without any indication that the first marriage ended as a result of fornication.

And, for those that think they will leave their spouse without Biblical justification and just date other people without marrying them, let me say that you are letting your lust deceive you into following a position that will cause much pain and hurt on your part, and probably hurt to others as well. Anyway, any persons who would date someone who they know is legitimately married to another must have questionable motives. And, if you are hiding the fact that you are married in order to get a date with someone, you are acting in a deceitful and selfish manner.

But, some of you may say: "What if my spouse says it is okay to go out on dates with someone?" From a practical standpoint, it is still not good for married folk to go out on a "date" with anyone but their spouse (please keep in mind the definition of a "date" used for this guideline as outlined earlier in the section entitled Dating Defined).

I once had a colleague who informed me about a date she was going on while her husband was away on a ski trip. When I expressed my shock that she was going "out on the town" with a man other than her husband, she assured me that all was okay and apparently this was how things were done in her marriage. Need I say that this dating practice of my colleague was a symptom of some severe problem in her marriage. Of no great surprise, my colleague eventually left her husband and started a family with some other man.

Please, people, follow God's will as revealed in the scripture. Don't try to out-maneuver the Bible as one woman did: while listening to a Christian radio program, the teacher explained how a lady was trying to get free of her husband. This lady concocted a plan to try and manipulate her husband into a situation where her husband would commit adultery. The lady had a friend who she knew was interested in her husband; the lady tried to orchestrate situations where the husband and her friend would be together. Let me warn you, that even if a person commits adultery, there is no guarantee that God will release the adulterer's spouse to divorce and date someone else. [This is by no means an endorsement for committing adultery. I am simply saying that God may judge the adulterer as well as judge the person who tries to get others to entice her husband, so she can have "just" cause to divorce her husband and date someone else.]

Now, if you do find yourself divorced as a result of your spouse engaging in sexual relationships outside of marriage, relationships that you did not try to orchestrate for the benefit of leading your spouse into sin, then I recommend that you seek professional counsel and let some time pass before jumping into the dating scene. Letting time pass is generally a good thing to do for more than one reason. You may find that your spouse is truly repentant after the divorce, and that he or she is willing to go through counseling and be accountable for not doing things that lead to infidelity. You may find that you desire to re-marry your former spouse after he or she has proven himself or herself honorable by behaving in a godly manner over an extended period of time.

Even if you never reconcile with your former spouse, you do risk the **appearance** of evil if you file for divorce in the morning and plan a date with another person the same afternoon. Be careful, it may appear as though you had a romantic relationship with someone else prior to the breakdown of your marriage. I am not saying you are sinning by having a date scheduled for the same afternoon that you file your divorce papers, but please consider what you do carefully.

Since you were most likely married in a community ceremony, I think it is only appropriate to make the Christian community aware that your marriage has ended in divorce as a result of adultery on your spouse's part. You don't have to give the general church a detailed commentary on the specifics of your spouse's affair. However, it is not wise to let the community find out first that you are dating, and then later down the line declare that you are legitimately divorced – it just causes confusion, and makes you and your date appear as adulterous church goers.

I know in this day and time, some people encourage children to date; I feel it is a mistake to push young kids into the grownup world of dating. Yes, the little boys and girls may have innocent little attractions to one another, but these children should not be burdened with the additional responsibilities of grownup male/female relationships when they have not even figured out who they are as a person. If a person is not of marrying age or approaching marriageable age, I really must question the intent of children going on dates. Let the kids have friends of both genders, let the kids of both genders play together in groups on the playground and at the park, let the kids of both genders attend each other's little birthday parties. However, there is no need for little 5 year old Jimmy to say he is "dating" little 4 year old Sally. And, for the sake of the children, stop asking the little boys: "Don't you have a girlfriend?" And, stop asking the little girls: "Don't you have a boyfriend?" Please quit this ridiculousness!

I am not saying that dating always leads to marriage, but it often does. So let's leave dating to the singles, as I have defined above.

country, racism is still prevalent despite the extremel
and widespread harm it can cause to communities.
are those attending church, teaching Bible class, e
who attempt to justify their racist views. So
listening to a live Christian radio broadcast,
called the program and shared how her ch
regarding whether it is okay for peopl
is so very sad, to find people so exp
of its contents. The first and fo
marrying) someone is that ea
Did you know that the patri
Look at the 12th Chapter

1 And Miria
the Ethio
marrie

2

that dating is
you are greatly mistaken. On the contrary.
individuals may enjoy and benefit from dating and should not be
ridiculed or laughed at – it is you who are ridiculous if you feel
that only the young have a monopoly on dating. By the same token,
these instructions on dating guidelines are also applicable to more
mature/senior dating individuals.

RACISM

It is amazing to me the wacky and dangerous ideas that sometimes
spring up amongst the Christian community. Unfortunately, in my

y destructive
Worse yet, there
ven church leaders,
me years ago, while
one of the radio listeners
urch was divided in belief
e to marry interracially. This
sed to the Bible, yet so ignorant
emost consideration in dating (or
ch of you are truly faithful to God.
arch Moses had an interracial marriage?
of the book of Numbers:

m and Aaron spake against Moses because of
pian woman whom he had married: for he had
d an Ethiopian woman.

And they said, Hath the LORD indeed spoken only by Moses? hath he not spoken also by us? And the LORD heard it.

3 (Now the man Moses was very meek, above all the men which were upon the face of the earth.)

4 And the LORD spake suddenly unto Moses, and unto Aaron, and unto Miriam, Come out ye three unto the tabernacle of the congregation. And they three came out.

5 And the LORD came down in the pillar of the cloud, and stood in the door of the tabernacle, and called Aaron and Miriam: and they both came forth.

6 And he said, Hear now my words: If there be a prophet among you, I the LORD will make myself known unto him in a vision, and will speak unto him in a dream.

7 My servant Moses is not so, who is faithful in all mine house.

8 With him will I speak mouth to mouth, even apparently, and not in dark speeches; and the similitude of the LORD shall he behold: wherefore then were ye not afraid to speak against my servant Moses?

9 And the anger of the LORD was kindled against them; and he departed.

10 And the cloud departed from off the tabernacle; and, behold, Miriam became leprous, white as snow: and Aaron looked upon Miriam, and, behold, she was leprous.

11 And Aaron said unto Moses, Alas, my lord, I beseech thee, lay not the sin upon us, wherein we have done foolishly, and wherein we have sinned.

12 Let her not be as one dead, of whom the flesh is half consumed when he cometh out of his mother's womb.

13 And Moses cried unto the LORD, saying, Heal her now, O God, I beseech thee.

14 And the LORD said unto Moses, If her father had but spit in her face, should she not be ashamed seven days? let her be shut out from the camp seven days, and after that let her be received in again.

15 And Miriam was shut out from the camp seven days: and the people journeyed not till Miriam was brought in again.

16 And afterward the people removed from Hazeroth, and pitched in the wilderness of Paran.

Did you know that Timothy, whom the Apostle Paul calls "my own son in the faith", was born to parents of differing backgrounds? Acts 16:1 and 2 says: "Then came he to Derbe and Lystra: and, behold, a certain disciple was there, named Timotheus, the son of a certain woman, which was a Jewess, and believed; but his father was a Greek: Which was well reported of by the brethren that were at Lystra and Iconium."

Nowhere, do I see Paul disparaging Timothy because his parents were of differing backgrounds. Quite the contrary: Paul entrusts Timothy with great responsibility and authority in helping him in spreading the gospel and teaching churches. This Timothy is the same one to whom Paul wrote the books of I and II Timothy.

Given our wicked world, there will likely be additional challenges if you and the person you wish to date are of different racial backgrounds. You may find that your seemingly loving church is filled with racists – from the pulpit to the usherboard. Your challenge then becomes whether you have the fortitude to oppose your church's racist, un-Biblical attitudes.

Now, I do realize that there are some parts of the world where dating someone outside of your racial background might place you or your date in mortal danger of attack by the unsaved community, or even in danger of governmental persecution. To you I say, seek God whether or not you should date that person. God can make a way for you to date, if it be His will. Even if God directs that you not date the person, know that he or she is your brother or sister in Christ and you are both equally part of God's family and kingdom.

Also know this: that there is no restriction on someone 55 years old dating someone who is 20 years old. It is permissible for you to date someone younger or older than you are. However, you must truly assess whether you are willing to deal with the extra challenges that may come your way with such a vast age difference. You must not only consider all possible challenges of dating someone with a vast age difference, but consider the challenges involved if you both decide to marry each other. You must think of the obvious potential long-range consequences before becoming so emotionally committed in a relationship.

Imagine that you are a man 20 years of age. If your date is 55 years old now and you develop a serious relationship and get married, when she is 70 years old you will only be 35 years old. As a much younger person, are you prepared to support your wife as she deals with the problems that are common to old age? It is highly probable that you will not be able to safely have children – are you willing to accept that fact?

MUST I BEAR CHILDREN?

Speaking of children, there once was a dear lady who held the belief that people should not get married and deliberately plan not to have children. Let me say that I do not hold to this belief. I feel that some improperly use Genesis 1:28 to support this belief. "And God blessed them, and God said unto them, Be fruitful, and multiply, and replenish the earth, and subdue it: and have dominion over the fish of the sea, and over the fowl of the air, and over every living thing that moveth upon the earth." Although most couples in the child-bearing years do and should expect to have children, it is a fallacy Biblically speaking to demand that couples should never date and marry unless they plan to have children.

I say this for multiple reasons.

First of all, the primary reason God gives for creating woman was "It is not good that the man should be alone..." (Genesis 2:18a)

Secondly, God's instruction to multiply and replenish the earth expressed God's desire that the earth be filled with people. With a world population that numbers in the billions, we have now reached a situation where certain nations are experiencing health crises due in part to overpopulation of specific geographic locations. Can we honestly say that God wants every couple of every nation to have as many children as possible?

Thirdly, it is quite clear that Paul was encouraging some to marry, regardless of their ability to have children. It appears that Paul encouraged marriage as a godly means for expressing one's sexual desire. "But if any man think that he behaveth himself uncomely toward his virgin, if she pass the flower of her age, and need so require, let him do what he will, he sinneth not: let them marry." (ICorinthians 7:36)

Also, look at I Corinthians 7:39: "The wife is bound by the law as long as her husband liveth; but if her husband be dead, she is at liberty to be married to whom she will; only in the Lord." This scripture deals with widows being free to remarry, only if they remarry a Christian man. It is quite obvious that Paul was instructing widows, even those past childbearing years, to marry if they so desired. In ITimothy 5: 9-11, Paul addresses a special position within the local church that was held by widows who would dedicate themselves entirely to church work. Paul instructs the church not to accept ladies to this position unless they are at least 60 years old. Those widows under 60 years were encouraged to marry. Obviously, those widows marrying in their 40s, 50s and beyond were not all marrying with the intent to have children.

Examine the passage for yourself:

9 Let not a widow be taken into the number under threescore years old, having been the wife of one man,

10 Well reported of for good works; if she have brought up children, if she have lodged strangers, if she have washed the saints' feet, if she have relieved the afflicted, if she have diligently followed every good work.

11 But the younger widows refuse: for when they have begun to wax wanton against Christ, they will marry;

NATIONAL AND PHYSICAL DIFFERENCES

Let's get back to my main thrust of individuals dating people with a different background.

There is no prohibition on dating someone of a different national origin. However, I do caution you to make sure that your date is not just interested in you as a way to prolong his or her stay in your country. I know that may sound really crude – but, this is a survival guide and I must give you all the tools I can to survive the dangers of dating.

Is it acceptable to date someone who is physically challenged (e.g., has lost his or her eyesight)?

There is no Biblical restriction against doing so. However, there may be some challenges to overcome in dating someone who is physically challenged.

NO ATTRACTION TO THE OPPOSITE SEX

A few Christians may have little or no interest/attraction to Christians of the opposite gender (see Matthew 19:12) – while at the same time, these individuals are not homosexuals, as they have no homosexual desires whatsoever. It is indeed quite possible for a man to lack the usual strong attraction to women, and for a woman not to be attracted to men, while possessing no homosexual tendencies. I find no prohibition against dating for these individuals with little or no attraction to prospective dates. However, I fear that if these special individuals date someone who is attracted to them, misunderstanding and hurt feelings may arise when it is discovered that the special individual has virtually no attraction to the opposite gender.

Let me pause here and say that attraction can be a variety of things (it is not necessarily the appeal of an "athletic" physique); you as a single person might become attracted to a Christian co-worker of the opposite gender because of the strength and integrity you have seen demonstrated in that person throughout trials you have experienced together. Or, maybe that young lady wears her hair just like your favorite high school math teacher.

Some of you may feel that you are not at all anxious to marry and wonder if you should date. It is perfectly okay (possibly preferable) not to be in a mad, desperate rush to find a marriage partner, for this might cause you to leap into a marriage commitment with the wrong person. However, if you are strongly adverse to ever getting married, my personal opinion is that you should consider not dating in this frame of mind – for the same reason that I give above, for an individual who has no attraction to the opposite gender. Maybe you should try going out or interacting with groups of people in the safe confines of non-date settings: you might find that you are not as adverse as you claim to be to the idea of marriage at some point in the future; then again, you may confirm your feeling that you don't ever want to marry – that is okay if you feel that way.

* * * * * * * * * * * * * * *

WHY DATE?

Within many (not all) cultures that I am familiar with, dating is the predominant process used to become more acquainted with people of the opposite gender and to determine one's selection of a marriage partner: to determine if that man is the desired choice for a husband, or to determine if that woman is the desired choice for a wife.

I believe that dating can be useful in selecting a marriage partner, as it gives a person a chance to learn his or her date's "real personality" by observing him or her in a variety of circumstances. With some people, on the first date you can begin to see indicators of the real personality. With other people, it takes longer to delve down and discover who they really are.

For example, a young man shows up for your first date with him; he knocks on the door and your father answers. Your father opens the door and your date addresses your father by saying: "Wassup, dog?" and walks past your father, right into the living room before your father even has a chance to say "Hello". I don't say that this young man sinned because he did not address the young lady's father appropriately; however, even on this first date, we seem to have encountered a young man uninstructed in what we call basic home training – this young man may need some extensive growth and mentoring before he's ready to venture into the dating arena.

[NOTE: "Wassup dog" is a very slang way of saying "Hello" to someone. This seems a very rude way to address someone.]

Another example: we might have a lady who is habitually no less than 30 minutes late for every date; over a period of time a Christian man might come to one of two conclusions: his date is a very disorganized person, or the young lady feels that the things that are making her late are more important than preventing the young man from having to wait 30 minutes (or more) for each date – this may, or may not, be a problem for the young man, depending upon the young man's expectations and the specific reasons why the young lady is always late (i.e., she is a doctor who frequently does on-call duty in the emergency room).

Again, it may take much time and quite a few experiences with your date to find out who she or he really is. It is the natural tendency of people to be on their best behavior until they become comfortable around the person whom they are dating. Whether consciously or unconsciously, some Christians turn into an entirely different person during the early part of their dating relationship. So, be observant as your dating with a particular person progresses over the course of months. Does he change from Dr. Jekyll into Mr. Hyde? Does she change from Cinderella to the Wicked Witch of the West? (Figuratively speaking, of course.) I am not saying that a person should be rude, inconsiderate, or wear their musty, old gardening clothes on the date. I am saying that you should not magically switch into some totally different person that even your family and closest friends do not recognize. Yes, you can grow and your personality can get better over time; however, don't be a phony changing back and forth like some sort of werewolf. (No, I don't believe in werewolves.)

How about a quick example of being observant: if your date's mother is totally shocked when he does small considerate things like open the door for her, this may be a hint that he usually does not open the door for his mother. Or, what if your date invites you to her parents' home for dinner, for a home cooked meal that your date prepared. When her little brother Jimmie sits down, he's amazed. Jimmie innocently exclaims: "I didn't know my sister even knew how to turn on the oven, 'cause I never seen her get near the kitchen except when mom is done fixin' the food!" Now, there may be a good and acceptable reason for this statement; and then again, maybe not. I am not suggesting that you carry around a little score-card on your dates that you pull out and add or remove points as you progress through each date. However, as you laugh, talk and enjoy your dates, you need to keep your wits about you and do the job of a psychologist, studying your date in his or her various interactions with you and interactions with other people over time. It may be that a person is a nice Christian, more suited to being your buddy than a potential spouse. Well, that's okay, you have gained a friend. Or, it may be that this person is not even suitable as a good friend; just keep your wits about you as different aspects of your date's personality are exposed to the light of day. And, it goes without saying: pray about your dates.

Okay, alright, I know some of you may be staunch advocates that when a person meets that special someone meant for them, they will hear golden bells, and see fireworks – somewhat of a "love at first sight" philosophy. I am not going to say that "love at first sight" can never happen, for I do know that God can speak to our hearts and reveal things to us instantaneously. But, we have too many falling quickly into what they call "true love", to later declare concerning their true love some statement, such as the following:

> There are a million and one things that I can't stand about him (or her).

Or, after people have married, how many times have you heard them say:

I made a Biiiiiiiiig Mistake!

It is better to make sure that what you think is true love is not just a superficial attraction (and your loneliness) causing your emotions to win out against wisdom and better judgment.

I want to emphasize in this guide that you should not assume that a person would make a good marriage partner because they are so physically attractive or are endowed with great talents. Many people who are attractive, gifted and famous have turned out to be the worst marriage partners and parents.

Do you remember King Solomon in the Bible?

Solomon was a successful builder and administrator – considered one of the greatest in history. However, you might not consider him a great example of a father and husband, even by Old Testament standards.

I Kings 11:1-3 says:

> 1 But king Solomon loved many strange women, together with the daughter of Pharaoh, women of the Moabites, Ammonites, Edomites, Zidonians, and Hittites;

> 2 Of the nations concerning which the Lord said unto the children of Israel, Ye shall not go in to them, neither shall they come in unto you: for surely they will turn away your heart after their gods: Solomon clave unto these in love.

> 3 And he had seven hundred wives, princesses, and three

hundred concubines: and his wives turned away his heart.

Talent and beauty did not provide a guarantee against Solomon exhibiting dysfunctional behavior in his interpersonal relationships – how awful of him to even consider having 700 wives.

Sometimes it is a person's very giftedness that leads them to believe that others must tolerate their ungodly behavior.

I once tried to convince someone who had been a Christian much longer than I, that even when a person initially accepts Christ, the person *possibly* still needs development and growth in his or her personality before he or she can make an acceptable marriage partner. I further tried to convince this Christian of my point by describing how a young man in the community may fall into the drug culture as a kid and basically go through his adolescent years "on the street", without the comfort of a solid home-life with good male role models. I am not saying such a young man will never make a good prospect for a date – but it is likely that such a young man will have to go through a period of intensive training and growth to learn the ways of healthy human relationships, even after becoming a Christian. The same would be true of an over-pampered young man from an affluent family who has led him to believe that the world revolves around him. And, there are cases between these two extremes. Individuals from these various backgrounds may truly accept Christ, but they will need to grow (see II Peter 3:18). Ah, but the dating process helps one to see those Christians who are not quite ripe enough to be picked.

DATING A HYPOCRITE

Also, you have some people who are fakes/hypocrites, who mix among the Christians. It is possible that you might accidentally find yourself on a date with one of these individuals. If you come to know that your date is not a Christian, do not proceed to a second date, as this is not best for your spiritual well being and might even be dangerous for your physical well being (i.e., some male and female hypocrites have violent tendencies). There is an old saying that goes something like this: "If he slapped you while you where dating, if you marry him he will kill you." I really believe there is much truth in this saying. There are certain traits that your date may reveal that will help you know to end the date immediately (and forevermore break off contact with the person); it depends on the gravity of what your date did .

I Corinthians 5:9-13 speaks about church people who brazenly/willfully sin, yet still profess to be Christians. God even authorizes the church leadership to put someone out of the church if his or her behavior becomes too unruly.

> 9 I wrote unto you in an epistle not to company with fornicators:
>
> 10 Yet not altogether with the fornicators of this world, or with the covetous, or extortioners, or with idolaters; for then must ye needs go out of the world.
>
> 11 But now I have written unto you not to keep company, if any man that is called a brother be a fornicator, or covetous, or an idolater, or a railer, or a drunkard, or an extortioner; with such an one no not to eat.
>
> 12 For what have I to do to judge them also that are without? do not ye judge them that are within?
>
> 13 But them that are without God judgeth. Therefore put away from among yourselves that wicked person.

Take a look at this same passage in The Living Bible (TLB), below:

> 9 When I wrote to you before I said not to mix with evil people.
>
> 10 But when I said that I wasn't talking about unbelievers who live in sexual sin, or are greedy cheats and thieves and idol worshipers. For you can't live in this world without being with people like that.
>
> 11 What I meant was that you are not to keep company with anyone who claims to be a brother Christian but indulges in sexual sins, or is greedy, or is a swindler, or worships idols, or is a drunkard, or abusive. Don't even eat lunch with such a person.
>
> 12 It isn't our job to judge outsiders. But it certainly is our job to judge and deal strongly with those who are members of the church, and who are sinning in these ways.
>
> 13 God alone is the Judge of those on the outside. But you yourselves must deal with this man and put him out of your church.

Later in this guide, when I explain how Christians are not to date non-Christians, I am including hypocrites in the category of a non-Christian. When you find out that someone is living the life of a hypocrite (even if they don't have violent/abusive tendencies), you should refrain from dating him or her based on the Biblical principle that Christians are not to date non-Christians.

Many of you know you are not supposed to date someone who is not a Christian. But I want to advise you not even to "hang out" with the person of the opposite sex who is obviously not a Christian. Some Christians fool themselves by saying "No! No, I would not develop a dating relationship with an unbeliever." Yet, they cling so tightly to that unsaved person of the opposite sex; they go the same places, do the same things just as though they were on a date. Don't fool yourself: if it walks like a duck, quacks like a duck, looks like a duck, flies like a duck – it is not a sparrow, it is a duck. Don't justify dating the wrong person by denying that you are going on what is in reality just a date.

HOW IS ANGER DISPLAYED?

There is a saying that you should have at least one big disagreement with a person before you get married. Now, I am not advocating that you pick a fight with your dates. However, be sure to observe how your date deals with anger when unpleasant things occur to him or her. Over time, some people tend to get relaxed with you and may reveal certain unhealthy tendencies.

Does your date resolve his or her anger by kicking or punching? If you are dating this type of person, you may try to defend him or her by saying that he or she never kicks or punches you. He or she only kicks or punches inanimate objects like the wall, or the door. You actually have some people who have holes in the walls of their house, which represent different times when they were so mad that they felt they just had to destroy something.

Well, he or she may not have slapped you yet, but if he or she is punching walls, you will get your serving by and by if you keep dating such a person.

You may say: "My date wouldn't dare slap me because he knows that I will shoot him with my gun if he does." Dear "Saint", what are you doing carrying around a concealed weapon, to shoot people who cross you? I believe that the Bible shows us that it would make us no less of a person to simply get away from the situation (even run if necessary), rather than carry weapons.

I say that if a person even threatens violent behavior (without actually doing anything) to intimidate his or her date, you have learned all that you need to know about your date: call the date off and break off the dating relationship.

If you are an observant and wise Christian, you will find that there are some relationships that you will not be able to hold onto – Samson in the book of Judges could provide you a really good testimony of the value of cutting off relationships that are pulling you away from God's will. In the 16th Chapter of the book of Judges, we see Samson falling in love with a woman named Delilah. Samson demonstrated great feats of physical strength while fighting against his enemy the Philistines. Samson was given this great strength by God; however, Samson was to be a Nazirite (especially dedicated to God), and Samson was not to cut his hair. The leaders of the Philistines offered Delilah money in order to entice Samson into revealing how he might be overcome. Day after day Delilah manipulated Samson until he finally told her how he might be defeated. Delilah lay Samson's head in her lap and lulled him to sleep. Samson soon found that his hair had been cut, God had departed from him, and his great strength was gone. The Philistines then easily overcame Samson, gouged out his eyes, and put him in prison.

But you say, you are trying to save the soul of your date, you feel that he or she needs to be helped. You are emotionally involved – if the person is really sincere, get that person together with one of your church elders or elderly spiritual ladies to council and minister to this person – and back way, way, way, way away from a relationship with the person. (Also, see the Holiness.com FireSide chat teaching on dating unsaved persons, included in the attachments section at the end of this book.)

DON'T BE TOO DESPERATE

Hey, you folks who love to fish: have you ever been fishing with someone who hooked into a large fish that just literally bent the pole over? After that guy or gal played that fish all the way to the edge of the boat, the fish may have simply rolled to one side and turned a flip and jumped right off the hook, swimming away to escape the frying pan. Didn't it look like the person wanted to dive in the water to get the fish? Maybe someone had to convince the person not to jump in, maybe even had to physically restrain him or her from jumping in that deep, dark, dangerous water? Well, no fish is worth risking the danger of jumping into murky, deep water and risking your life. In like manner, no date is worth throwing away prudence and reason to jump into an obviously dangerous relationship.

Be careful about being so desperate to get married or have a date that you give your date (or potential date) the impression that you are desperate. Selfish people will use this knowledge to take advantage of you and honorable people will think that something must be wrong with you, that you would be so desperate. It is okay to reveal that you like your date, but don't do like one date I had: I met this young lady through a friend. She and I had possibly two or three conversations on the phone. At one point, we agreed to meet at a mutually agreeable public event, a special service being held by her family at a church in my city. When I arrived at the service, I was directed to where my date sat as we had only talked on the phone and had never met in person. After sitting down and greeting my date, it seemed that less than two minutes passed before my date pounced on me with a question. She said: "Well, what do you think?" Trying to figure out where this was going, I asked: "About what?" Then she said, rather matter-of-factly: "About me". I felt like a deer caught in the headlight of a Big Mack Truck, and I didn't like the feeling. I then nicely told the young lady that I sort of liked to get to know a person (i.e., before making a judgment about a person). She then snapped back at me, in a very agitated tone, that she didn't believe in playing games because she was looking to get married. I sat there in shock, as if she had just harpooned me in the chest. Need I say that I never called her again.

Some situations are not quite so dramatic as the previous date I mentioned: there was a beautiful young lady that I briefly met through a relative and later saw her around town several times. Some time later, this young lady, whom I did not really know well at all, called me on the telephone. She obviously obtained my telephone number without my knowledge. I don't advise that you surreptitiously obtain the telephone number of someone who does not know you well and then "cold-call" them. And, if you insist that you feel you should do this, one of the first things from your lips should be an apology for calling the person this way. Also, express that you hope you have not offended them in calling them this way. Even if the person is glad that you called, your offering an apology will let the person being called know that you respect their privacy and that you don't want to be pushy (that you have good "home training").

Unfortunately, after a few phone conversations with my young beautiful caller, she began demanding to know where I was, if per chance I happened not to be home whenever she called. Ladies and Gentlemen, don't close in on your prospective date like he or she is a trapped wild animal and you are a hunter who has not eaten fresh meat in weeks. It's somewhat of an art to show interest in your date, but not to smother your date to death (so to speak). Keep your eyes wide open, and if you make a mistake by being too pushy, know how to back up a little (very gently). Some people back up so far, they give a false/incorrect impression of being cold and snobbish.

DATING AS AN IDOL GOD

There is a Biblical truth that I think I should mention. Did you know that anything can be an idol god? Most of the time people envision an idol god as some ugly little statue that people bow down to and offer sacrifices to. However, an idol god can be anything – anything that you desire more than your relationship with God.

Has Dating become your god? Do you sacrifice all reason and appropriate behavior just to get a date for that special event coming up? Are you unable to get into the worship service for always watching the door for potential love interests? Let the ushers watch the door and you should get into the worship, not gawk at every pretty face that comes in the door.

You can enjoy much spiritual fellowship in dating other committed Christians. But, dating is not a replacement for God.

Are you so engrossed in dating that you regularly take foolish risks? For example, you want to go on a picnic with your date and the time you have chosen conflicts with your work schedule; so, you call your boss and say that you won't be in to the office today because you are sick.

Are you constantly on the phone at work talking to your dates, making plans with your dates, and talking about your dates with friends? Has it gotten to the point where you are in danger of being fired because your work is not getting done and that work which you do is grossly substandard?

Are you skipping important classes, causing your grades to be poor, or missing assignments, or tests; neglecting your chores and responsibilities at your home to the point that your family members are suffering? Are you doing this because you are spending too much time dating?

Are you regularly up late at night talking with your date so much so that you fall asleep while in church? Or, do you sit up in church, oblivious to what is going on around you, because you are always daydreaming about your date?

Be careful, you just might be on your way to idol worship. A relationship that causes you to do so poorly at work that you get fired, does not sound like a positive relationship. You may think that you can live on Love, but when the glow fades you are going to need money to live in this present world (short of divine miracles).

Yes, I understand that romantic feelings are powerful feelings, and that these feeling can be intoxicating. But God does not mean for Christians to be drunk and disorderly and to cause our employer (or others) to see a poor representation of what it is to be a Christian.

But, you say "I am bored and there is nothing else to do but go on dates, plan for dates, think about dates, dream about dates...." You are imbalanced. Maybe you need a hobby. The sole purpose for living is not to go on a date. Don't be consumed with dating; be consumed with God.

Furthermore, let me say that anyone who would even desire to replace God in your life is not a good person to develop a dating relationship with. When you date these types of people, you may find them hindering you from attending church regularly. You may find this type of a person trying to cut you off totally from healthy Christian friends. He or she may even prevent you from having a healthy relationship with your family. He or she simply wants to be the center of your universe, and may not want you to have any other relationships that might interfere with what he or she desires. Run (don't walk) from a person with a god-like complex.

You go to a Bible-based church and have healthy Christian friends, yet your date is trying to cut you off from all relationships – danger!

DANGER! **DANGER!** Run (don't walk) from a person with a god-like complex.

Okay, so maybe you have not made an idol god out of your dating, nor of your desire to go on dates. But, you should be careful about letting someone you are only dating (not married to) become the most important human in your life. It is a bad choice to pour all your trust and emotional dependence into someone to the exclusion and rejection of every other wholesome relationship (e.g., family, and Christian friends). Some who have dysfunctional families may pour everything into that guy or girl, due to a lack of family and friends.

A date should be an enhancement to the life that you have, not the replacement of every other human relationship (e.g., Father, Mother, Sister, Brother, Pastor, etc.).

CHRISTIANS, BUT INCOMPATIBLE

If I have said it once, I have said it a hundred times: a person can be a Christian and still not be the best selection of a spouse for you.

Let me give you a parable of two people who are saved but may simply be incompatible:

> Let's say we have an intelligent Christian lady who has established a business and built it into a multi-million dollar operation. Let's say she starts going out on dates with a handsome, suave Christian man who thinks he is extremely knowledgeable regarding handling finances. On each of their dates, the man always insists on going somewhere expensive and flashy for dinner (despite the young lady voicing her strong objections each and every date). The Christian lady notices over a period of time that the man seems to have at least 12 different credit cards. And, each time the man offers

to pay for dinner, the young lady feels a strong urge to slip away to the restroom and hide; 50% of the time that he pays for something, the first 2 or 3 credit cards he offers for the purchase are rejected (purchase declined) before he finds a credit card with enough credit available to make the purchase (the man has even been asked by a credit card company to turn in his card to a merchant during a date). However, the man always insists all is going great with his financial affairs and strongly refuses the lady's offer to refer him to a credit counselor she knows, who does counseling for free. This lady may unnecessarily be risking her financial success by continuing to move forward in a dating relationship with this gentleman. Can a man be saved and be an incompetent steward of his financial affairs? Yes, indeed.

But, you say, you are certain that he or she is the one, because you heard a voice from heaven, and you had a dream, and you had an open vision, and three friends confirmed that he or she is the one through a word of prophecy. Okay, he or she might be the one. However, if God shows you your dream-house would it always be a sin to still do a walk-through (i.e., walk around in the house and on the property to see what you're buying)? And, might you have to come to an agreement/understanding regarding the final details of the purchase with the seller of the house before you sign on the dotted line?

In like manner, it might be advisable for you to date your dream-man/woman until you get some things worked through. (e.g., getting an understanding with your future husband as to what mutually agreeable financial practices are that you can both live by. If your expectation is that a mother should not have to work outside the home until the children are all school-age, this expectation should not arise in discussion for the first time after you have married.)
It is easy to hear voices and see visions while you're blinded by the prospect of that luscious man (or woman) being all yours in the

bliss of holy matrimony. I by no means want you to doubt God, or hesitate when God is saying make a move immediately; however, it is a fact that so many who thought they heard God have later confessed that it was really not God who was speaking. Be very careful about saying that God said something that you simply want to be God's will.

And, remember this: when God first shows you your dream house, he may still want you to step back and wait while He fixes the leaking roof, the bad plumbing, the termite and rat infestation, etc. Do you get my point? You not only must do what God says to do, but you must do it according to his timing, and exactly in the manner God wants you to.

MAKING GOOD FRIENDS

Another benefit to dating is making some very good friends. Even if you never find that marriage partner of your dreams, dating the right caliber of people allows you to enjoy people while establishing good and wholesome relationships with Christian brothers and sisters. Of course, when you do decide to marry (or commit yourself to just dating that one special someone prior to making a marriage promise), you will no longer date the various individuals that you have befriended over the course of your life, but it is possible to maintain a sisterly or brotherly friendship with these Christian brothers and sisters.

In addition to meeting nice people and possibly developing some good friendships, dating is one of the ways in which some people are able to better refine what they were looking for in a spouse. Have you ever heard a Christian man who said something like: "All I want is a woman who has a shapely figure and dresses well." Or, maybe you have heard a Christian lady say: "All I want is a man who has curly hair, and a nice car." Through interactions with the opposite sex, individuals will sometimes develop a more complete picture of what it is he or she really needs in a spouse to be happy in marriage. (see both parts 1 and 2 of <u>What the Christian Man is Looking for in a Woman</u> in the attachments at the end of this book).

Sometimes, one learns things about himself or herself on a date (e.g., you may have never known that you would like miniature golf so much, until you found yourself on a date enjoying miniature golf). Or, you may learn that your favorite cologne, which you feel is so captivating, really is overpowering to the point that your date very diplomatically suggests that it would be economical if you put a little less on. Or, you may learn that you love Creole cuisine while at a Southern-style dinner with your date. Or, you may find that you love horseback riding while at the church picnic.

UNDESIRABLE REASONS FOR DATING

Although there are possibly some additional good reasons to date that are of less importance, I would like to turn your attention to some reasons for going on a date, which are not very desirable.

In the non-Christian world, all too many individuals date with the intent to fulfill their burning passion outside the sanctity of marriage; there are some individuals who attempt to do the same thing within the Christian dating circle. Need I say that this is a bad reason to date.

Although it is not necessarily wrong to desire to date individuals who are financially secure, be careful not to become a Church gigolo. What I am getting at here is that some people date primarily to obtain financial gain (or other advantage) from people. These church gigolos literally do not care about the welfare of the people that they use to get what they want.

Let me give you a parable:

> Sarah has a gigantic crush on (i.e., strong attraction to) the church drummer, Jim. Jim does not have any attraction to Sarah, and quite honestly hates going on dates with her. However, Sarah has a new sports car, and by dating Sarah, Jim is able to convince her to allow him to borrow her car when she is not using it. Jim even takes other young ladies on dates in Sarah's car (without Sarah's knowledge). When Sarah feels compelled to sell the sports car and buy a used station wagon (Sarah is struggling to finance her college education), we find that Jim is no longer willing to go on dates with Sarah. As a matter of fact, Jim never again bothers to even call Sarah, or send a Birthday card or Christmas card. "Mysteriously," Jim becomes suddenly enamored with Sarah's cousin, Debra, who just bought a convertible.

Some people use dating strictly as a tool to gain some advantage that the other person has to offer. This type of dating takes a variety of forms:

> - an unscrupulous church person might date a Christian manager only to attempt to influence the Christian manager to hire the church person for a job that has recently been vacated.

> - or, maybe a Christian brother or sister is acquainted with well-known ministers and gospel music artists; some shallow church people would be tempted to date this Christian brother or sister only to meet the "famous" people that the Christian brother or sister is capable of introducing them to. I could go on and on with examples of this type, but I won't.

Some people date simply because all (or most) of their friends are dating. Although it is not necessarily a sin to date for this reason, it strikes me as a very immature reason for dating.

Some people prescribe to soap opera dating: Craig goes on dates with Sally; Sally really likes Craig; Craig does not enjoy dating Sally; Craig really wants to date Jane; Jane somewhat likes Craig, but is dating Bo right now; so, Craig is only dating Sally to make Jane jealous, because Craig knows that Jane and Sally don't get along the best. You may think this type of stuff never happens in the church, but I was once in a serious relationship with a young lady (years and years ago) who heard from a friend that I was seen somewhere with another woman. The young lady with whom I was in a committed relationship had mutually agreed with me that we would date only each other. When the young lady approached me with the accusation of being on a date with someone else, I of course vehemently denied this false accusation. She obviously did not believe me, as she went on a date with another young man (unbeknownst to me), and was foolish enough to tell me about her date afterward and how the young man insinuated/teased that he wanted to marry her. It was obvious to me that she was trying to cause me pain and hurt for something that I was not even guilty of (her incorrect information that I took some other lady on a date).

Do I need to tell you that this relationship quickly disintegrated. Love triangles are not God's way. As for trying to "get even" (or exact revenge), the Bible says (in Romans 12:19): "Dearly beloved, avenge not yourselves, but rather give place unto wrath: for it is written, Vengeance is mine; I will repay, saith the Lord." If someone you are dating is behaving dishonestly with you, a "Love Triangle" (or Love Square or Octagon) is not the solution; it may be best to calmly and quickly end the dating relationship with the dishonest person. You see, if the young lady in my case had not been so quick to be vengeful and un-Christlike, she might have more wisely and calmly investigated the accusation against me. And, even if she had decided to break off our relationship, she would have maintained her integrity and we might have reconciled at some later time once she learned the real truth of her "friend's" accusation.

As I considered the demise of this particular relationship years later, I do recall the day (on which I allegedly was on a date with someone else) was an occasion where my parents and I had given a middle-aged mother in the church a ride from our church to an afternoon service at our sister church. I can assure you that I was not on a date with this saintly mother (who is older than both my parents), and is more like a mother figure to me. I guess it goes to show you that if you live for the Lord, he can beautify the senior women to the point that they make the young ladies jealous (although, the ~~lying~~ gossiping lips of my date's "friend" did not help the situation either).

Some individuals date because other people are pressuring them to date. Unfortunately, some people in the church feel that it is their self-proclaimed responsibility to go around the church congregation and match up all of the single Christians into couples, (whether or not all of the single individuals desire to date at all). I can recall years ago when I was struggling to make it through undergraduate school; if you bugged me then about when I was getting married, I might have been tempted to say "when I get a job". At that time in my life, I just don't know if I could have personally handled the additional distraction and pressure of going on very many dates. If you are one of those self-proclaimed ~~busybodies~~ matchmakers, please be careful that you are not providing your services to unwilling customers. (There's nothing like someone trying to sell/give you a piano and you have no desire whatsoever to play.) I am sure many of you can recognize the insensitive type of matchmaker that too often runs loose in the church, but let me provide some parables anyway, to help those of you who are unwittingly offending people who are too kind to tell you that you have become a nuisance:

In our first parable, we have Raul, who is a quiet, handsome, well mannered, single Christian man in his mid-forties. He decides to visit the Christian church that one of his male co-workers belongs to. Upon entering the church, a good number of the ladies in the front of the church begin eyeing him like a wolf-pack about to devour a poor little bunny rabbit. Raul feels somewhat uncomfortable about being watched so closely, but manages to enjoy the very sound message put forward by the Pastor. After the service is over, Raul's co-worker tells Raul to have a seat in a pew at the rear of the church while he runs and gets a first-time visitor package/gift for Raul. In the instant that Raul's co-worker steps away, Sister Bocado (the Pastor's Aunt), quickly approaches Raul, introduces herself, and asks Raul if he is married. Raul frowns ever so slightly, but begrudgingly admits that he is not married. Sister Bocado turns toward the front of the church where the wolf-eyed ladies stand chit-chatting, then shouts very loudly: "Hey, girls; yawl better come on down, this here's a single man!" At this point, Raul feels like crawling under the seat.

If you think things like this don't happen, you just haven't been around enough. Never, never, let yourself be guilty of needlessly embarrassing an unmarried person due to such insensitive matchmaking. It would have been a much better approach if Sister Bocado would have discreetly whispered to Raul's co-worker if he would mind introducing Raul to some of the young ladies; and then to let things take a more natural course.

Or, we have the parable of the hard-working young lady, let's call her Ruth, who scrimped and saved enough to buy a car. Deacon Milo, who's been trying to marry off his lazy nephew, asks Ruth if she could perform a humanitarian assignment for him next Saturday afternoon, now that she has been blessed with a car. Ruth, who has known Deacon

Milo all her life, trustingly says: "Sure, I'd be glad to. What's the assignment?"(Ruth has in her mind that some mother needs a ride to the grocery store, or some such other little errand.) Deacon Milo, muttering and stammering, asks Ruth: "It would mean a whole lot to me personally if you would take my nephew to the Pastor's annual Award's Banquet." Now, the look of horror on Ruth's face should have been enough to cause Deacon Milo to gracefully retract the request; but he continues: "You know, I have always been there for you when you needed me. And, this would be a big favor to me…"

I am afraid there are sometimes no easy way to get out of these situations other than respectfully telling the person that you love them and respect them, but that you would prefer they not put you in such an uncomfortable situation. I feel justified in saying that dating someone is usually not supposed to be motivated out of favors that you owe a third party. I once had someone very dear to me try to "prophesy me" into dating someone whom I had already come to know to be a "WILD TIGRESS".

Some of the insensitive matchmakers might defend their draconian (barbaric) styled approach of introducing singles by citing those who have married through their tactics. However, to be fair and balanced, we need to see how many mess-ups they have made (e.g., people needlessly made to feel so embarrassed that they wanted to crawl into a hole and disappear, or worse, couples put on a fast-track to the wedding altar who later find that they should have waited before making a marriage commitment).

I recommend a person sit down in thought and prayer before jumping into the dating scene, to determine his or her motivation for dating in general. I would also recommend before dating a particular person, that you pray about your choice of a date and ask yourself the question: "why am I going on a date with this person?" If by praying and asking this question, you don't come up with godly answers, maybe you should not pursue this particular date.

* * * * * * * * * * * * * * *

WHAT? AND HOW?

What are appropriate activities and places to enjoy on a date, and how should one act when dating?

As I have mentioned before, dating someone provides an opportunity to get to know someone more closely. As you begin dating someone, I believe it is important to establish some ground rules fairly early in your dating of that person. For example, you may have correctly surmised that "necking" (e.g., intense, passionate kissing) is something that unmarried people should not do. However, your date may believe that it is "okay" (even "good") to do. Thus, to avoid being surprised much later down the road, it is important early in the dating to make sure that you and your date are both clear on the ground rules (e.g., no necking).

Now, I am not suggesting that you have your date read a list of all your dating rules and sign the bottom in blood before going on your first date.

You may need to introduce certain subjects subtly and wisely, so as not to seem accusatory (i.e., when trying to get across that you don't "make out", go "necking" or any such passionate physical contact).

Consider this: if you have agreed to go on a date and feel nervous that maybe you will run out of things to say or discuss on your date, I have a solution to that problem. I can almost guarantee you that you won't run out of things to discuss, if you take this book along as a discussion starter. Maybe mention this book to your prospective date and indicate that you would like to get his or her opinion on certain parts of the book.

If your date is honest as you discuss the book, I would think that this would assist you in getting to know your date more than sitting around talking about the weather (unless you are dating a meteorologist).

Unfortunately, some Christians think that they are under some special dispensation of grace when it comes to dating and that it is acceptable to act in a manner that does not bring glory to God. Every Christian needs to understand that God commands us to live a life of Holiness (Biblical Holiness); this way of life is not just for Sundays, but must permeate the very nature of who we are – 24 hours a day, 365 days a year (and even the extra day during leap year).

In dating relationships, a Christian can bring glory to God by behaving in a manner that is not selfish, but considerate of his or her date; the verse that comes to mind is Philippians 2:3: "Let nothing be done through strife or vainglory: but in lowliness of mind let each esteem other better than themselves." If you truly esteem/value your date, the date's Christian relationship with God will be greatly regarded: this great regard should be apparent by your conscious effort not to do or say things that would tend to tempt your date to do anything that would be displeasing to God. So, there you have it: one should be considerate of (not selfish toward) his or her date, and one should value his or her date's Christian relationship with God.

Before we speak more about how Christ-like attributes should affect a Christian's dating habits, let me share what may be totally new concepts for some of you.

The first concept is the principle that God expects both men and women, boys and girls to wait until after marriage to experience physical intimacy. There are all sorts of expressions floating around that are meant to excuse the promiscuity of men; phrases such as "boys will be boys". This phrase, and all such lines of reasoning, are not only foolish, but dangerous to the eternal souls of men who attempt to rationalize their promiscuous behavior with such phrases.

I Corinthians 6:9 says: "Know ye not that the unrighteous shall not inherit the kingdom of God? Be not deceived: neither fornicators, nor idolators, nor adulterers, nor effeminate, nor abusers of themselves with mankind".

The first principle above naturally leads to a second principle: it is not only important that ladies guard against being led into fornication, but men should also guard against being led into the sin of fornication. Could this at least be partly what Apostle Paul had in mind when he told his apt student Timothy to "Flee also youthful lusts: but follow righteousness…"? (II Timothy 2:22)

But you say that it is so much more exciting to be promiscuous, just like romance is portrayed in most movies. Well, I cannot deny the point that loose living has its pleasure. But, ultimately someone will assuredly suffer extremely unpleasant consequences as the result of living a life that is not chaste (this goes for males and females). Furthermore, ungodly movies should not be the role model that we are seeking to follow. I know that living chastely can be a challenge, but the challenge is made even greater when we Christians spend our time soaking up ungodly movies that promote ungodly principles. Some people boldly proclaim that "these romance movies don't phase me, they have no impact on my behavior or thoughts". Sure, right, and I would like to ask one of these persons if they also believe the moon is made of Swiss Cheese.

Movies (and other mass means of communication, such as radio or even books) are tools that can be used to introduce ideas that influence a society or community toward a righteous direction, or toward an unrighteous direction. Ungodly concepts, portrayed over and over, that promote promiscuity, without any doubt, has had a negative influence on the thoughts and actions of generation after generation.

APPROPRIATE PHYSICAL CONTACT

Okay, so you say that you've got the point that it is not God's will for people to fornicate. But, you still may be wondering how much physical contact you should/shouldn't have with your date. Opinions in the world today run the gamut, from those that feel one should not get within 10 feet of their date, to those wrapped so tightly and intently around each other, they appear at a quick glance to be wrestling. Some people feel that as long as those dating keep their clothes on they can handle each other however they want without being guilty of sin. Boy, oh boy! That is like saying you can kiss a venomous cobra on the mouth without getting bitten; that may be, but I don't recommend kissing cobras.

Any time you try to sexually fulfill yourself with another person with whom you are not married (clothes on, or clothes off), you are SINNING. There is a passage of scripture that comes to mind that is not necessarily directly related to dating, but it triggers an interesting point in my mind: I Timothy 5:2 says: "The elder women as mothers; the younger as sisters, with all purity." Paul was telling Timothy to treat/respect the Christian women in some degree as he would women of his own blood family. What I am trying to get at here is the idea that just because you are dating someone, you do not have a right to take lots of extra privileges in your physical contact with your date. That date is still to be given the respect that you would give for the physical person of someone in your blood family who you highly respect. Even if you are engaged to be married, and you love each other ever so deeply, that is not sufficient justification to act as if your bodies belong to each other. Your physical bodies do not belong to each other until and AFTER you perform your marriage vows; not the night before your wedding, or not even one second before the wedding.

On occasion, Christians may break off a wedding engagement; it is not necessarily a sin to break off an engagement. But, if you have been sleeping with your fiancé (or fiancée), God is not happy, and one or both of you should feel that you have cheated yourself and each other out of waiting until your special wedding night. Also, the professional marriage experts have determined that people who have sexual relations with each other before marriage, are much more likely to cheat on each other after marriage. Christian Author and Counselor, James L. Christensen, discusses the evidence (such as the famous Kinsey report) which shows a relationship between premarital sex and infidelity after marriage in his book *Before Saying "I Do"*.

Love (or should I say lust) should never be used as an excuse to sin. If your date willfully disregards his Love for Christ and will commit fornication with you outside of marriage because he or she "Loves" you so much, what makes you think he or she will not commit adultery after you marry him or her, with the next person whom he or she finds and loves more than God and you?

A few of you may have somewhat peculiar notions of what respect you should have for the physical person of some greatly-respected person in your blood family. So, let me provide some additional explicit examples to clarify things a bit.

I do not wrestle with my granny (grandmother). So, according to the guideline that I have given above, our dating couple above who have their bodies wrapped so tightly and intently around each other in fun and play, would not be viewed as respecting each other's physical person as defined by our guideline.

Some folks who date look as if they are giving each other mouth-to-mouth resuscitation (yet no one is drowning; neither person even fell in the water). This is not respectful of one's date.

It has been a long, long, long time since I was young enough for it to seem appropriate for me to sit in Granny's lap. Suffice it to say, you should not be sitting in your date's lap.

Would my granny take me by the hand, and maybe even pat my hand? Yes, she would and I would say it is not inappropriate to take your date by the hand if you both so desire and feel that your dating has progressed to a very serious level. However, there are probably so few other places you should pat your date prior to marriage.

I see little reason for one to massage the chest of their date; not unless your date has had legitimate heart failure (i.e., your date has fallen out in the middle of the restaurant during your evening together) and you are certified to perform cardiopulmonary resuscitation. Come to think of it, even the preacher should be extra discreet in how and where he "lays on hands" when he is praying for ladies of the church (or when church ladies pray for men).

Although more freedom is given as for the manner in which a man might pray for a man, or a woman might pray for a woman, it is still advisable to exercise some caution as to avoid violating someone's personal space, and to avoid being accused of homosexuality. Even a false accusation of homosexuality can cause great harm to someone's reputation.

Since we are pulling the cover off inappropriate behavior, let me also mention that I used to know young ladies who would "accidentally" trip and find themselves sitting in some young man's lap. Ladies and Gentlemen, be careful; I would like to suggest that you look where you are walking and pay attention to what you are doing, so that we might prevent these so called "accidents."

Or, there is the old crusty and over-used tactic of <u>trying to get something from your date</u>. It works like this: your date playfully snatches an object from you (e.g., your bracelet, your hat, a penny); you and your date then end up wrapped around each other "wrestling" over the object. I am all for fun and play, but I cannot think of a good and godly reason for a single man and a single woman to be tightly wrapped around each other in "play". Wait until you are married and then you can "play", pinch, pat, and tickle your beloved to your heart's content.

The thing that leaves me so puzzled is that some church folk who date can hardly keep their hands off each other before the wedding; but not many years after the wedding, some cannot even stand the sight of each other.

Proverbs 6:27 and 28 immediately come to mind: "Can a man take fire in his bosom, and his clothes not be burned? Can one go upon hot coals, and his feet not be burned?" Well, before one reaches the point of what the dictionary (or a court of law) defines as "fornication", one can reach a point of physical contact that still should only be between husband and wife. If dating individuals participate in this type of physical contact, you can count on being burned by some negative consequences associated with this risky and dangerous behavior. Even if no immediate ill consequences result, your passion will be ignited to the point that it is extremely hard to maintain purity in your dating relationship.

No, I won't define and describe every conceivable type of improper physical contact. But, hopefully the direction given in this guideline gives you enough information to know that you should not attempt to fulfill and gratify your passion with your date physically, neither by engaging in what the dictionary defines as fornication, nor by engaging in practices that technically (according to man's tricky reasoning) don't constitute "actual" fornication, as defined in a court of law.

DANGEROUS TALK

Some of you might be saying right now that you would never touch your date inappropriately as defined above; this is commendable that you say this. However, I want to give you some additional tips to reflect on. Please recall what we said earlier, concerning your making a "conscious effort not to do or say things that would tend to tempt your date to do anything that would be displeasing to God". Many times it is not just the sensory perception of touch that can cause temptation, it is sometimes what people say that can cause temptation.

You may talk quite often on the telephone with individuals that you date. And, your date might be in the privacy of his or her home during your phone conversation, maybe while sitting in his or her underclothing in his or her bedroom. What good does it do (in preventing temptation) to have long, in-depth discussions in your phone conversation as to the specific details of his or her underclothing (what they look like, size, etc.)

Another danger to watch out for is getting into extremely detailed discussions with your date regarding promiscuous activities that you might have taken part in during your past. I would dare say that some specific details of your past sins are not even necessary for your spouse to know. Yes, if you have been promiscuous in the past, you might tell your fiancé/fiancée something general such as "I have not always maintained purity in my dating relationships of the past, but since accepting Christ as my Savior I have been living pure before the Lord".

By no means am I recommending that you give your fiancé/fiancée, nor even your spouse, a detailed account of all the wicked deeds of your past; nor an account of everyone involved in those acts; nor a score-card comparing your past dates to your spouse once you become married. This type of disclosure tends to cause someone to get angry and upset, or tends to cause excitement to a level of passion that is dangerous at hearing such salacious details.

I know of a couple that wrongly fell into a sinful and egotistical contest of trying to top each other: each person successively took turns trying to out-do each other, trying to see who could recount the most lustful act they had personally performed in their past – well, this foolish game ended in a huge fight.

I am also aware of a woman who felt guilty concerning her secret affair with another woman's husband within her community. This woman stood up publicly to confess her sin during the church's testimony service – she intended to also name the man in her testimony with whom she had the secret affair; most fortunately, the lady was prevented from dropping such a bombshell (lusty, formerly-hidden sin) in her testimony/confession in the presence of all parishioners young and old, strong minded and weak.

Don't play dangerous games. Some people try to get away with saying certain improper things by laughing while they make improper statements.

Let me give you a parable:

Brad pulls his car to a stop and parks in front of his date's home. As she gets in the car, she sits down with a strange smirk on her face. Brad asks, "What's so funny?" The lady (Jenny) says: "You know that very expensive Hotel at the end of Marina Beach? Well, I just won a coupon for a free two-night stay; an entire suite for tonight and tomorrow night." Jenny laughs mischievously and says in a light-hearted fashion: "Why don't you and I use the coupon after dinner?"

Brad then grins slightly, winks one eye at Jenny, and with a deep, low, overly theatrical voice, says: "Oh my dove; Just you and me, the night, and the sound of the waves. Why don't we just skip the restaurant? We can order dinner in the suite."

Now, this game may be foolish jesting, or it may be a coy way of suggesting a dangerous idea where either party can avoid embarrassment by denying that they were serious if the other party becomes offended by the suggestion. You have some cases where individuals "humorously" suggest fornication and then accuse the innocent party of not having a sense of humor when the innocent party becomes offended by the "humorous" suggestion. In either case, I recommend you don't play like this unless you are married to the person you are playing with.

Ephesians 5:3-4 says: "But fornication, and all uncleanness, or covetousness, let it not be once named among you, as becometh saints; Neither filthiness, nor foolish talking, nor jesting, which are not convenient: but rather giving of thanks." The Living Bible (TLB) paraphrases this scripture as follows: "Let there be no sex sin, impurity or greed among you. Let no one be able to accuse you of any such things. Dirty stories, foul talk and coarse jokes – these are not for you. Instead, remind each other of God's goodness and be thankful." Philippians 4:8 says: "Finally, brethren, whatsoever things are true, whatsoever things are honest, whatsoever things are just, whatsoever things are pure, whatsoever things are lovely, whatsoever things are of good report; if there be any virtue, and if there be any praise, think on these things."

Instead of using laughter, some people use their date's pity to place their date into a compromising situation. For example, a person may have fallen on hard times in the past, or possibly has recently experienced a tragedy. The person who has fallen on hard times may ask the date to come over and cook for them or perform some other favor. The date, being a compassionate person, wants to comply with the person's request in an effort to bring some comfort in the time of sorrow. However, the key thing that should set off alarms in the mind of the date is the fact that the grieving person wants the date to come alone. And, once alone, the date will inevitably find himself or herself in a situation where the grieving person wants to be consoled with physical affection. Do I need to explain further, the danger of this situation?

As horrible and despicable as this tactic is, Amnon uses a very similar ploy when he assaults Tamar in II Samuel, chapter 13. Amnon's deeds are so appalling that I started not to include the text of the scriptural reference (II Samuel 13:1-19). Yet, this book may be read by those who do not own a Bible, so I reluctantly include the passage below:

> 1 And it came to pass after this, that Absalom the son
> of David had a fair sister, whose name was Tamar; and
> Amnon the son of David loved her.
>
> 2 And Amnon was so vexed, that he fell sick for his sister
> Tamar; for she was a virgin; and Amnon thought it hard
> for him to do any thing to her.
>
> 3 But Amnon had a friend, whose name was Jonadab, the
> son of Shimeah David's brother: and Jonadab was a very

subtil man.

4 And he said unto him, Why art thou, being the king's son, lean from day to day? wilt thou not tell me?
And Amnon said unto him, I love Tamar, my brother Absalom's sister.

5 And Jonadab said unto him, Lay thee down on thy bed, and make thyself sick: and when thy father cometh to see thee, say unto him, I pray thee, let my sister Tamar come, and give me meat, and dress the meat in my sight, that I may see it, and eat it at her hand.

6 So Amnon lay down, and made himself sick: and when the king was come to see him, Amnon said unto the king, I pray thee, let Tamar my sister come, and make me a couple of cakes in my sight, that I may eat at her hand.

7 Then David sent home to Tamar, saying, Go now to thy brother Amnon's house, and dress him meat.

8 So Tamar went to her brother Amnon's house; and he was laid down. And she took flour, and kneaded it, and made cakes in his sight, and did bake the cakes.

9 And she took a pan, and poured them out before him; but he refused to eat. And Amnon said, Have out all men from me. And they went out every man from him.

10 And Amnon said unto Tamar, Bring the meat into the chamber, that I may eat of thine hand. And Tamar took the cakes which she had made, and brought them into the chamber to Amnon her brother.

11 And when she had brought them unto him to eat, he took hold of her, and said unto her, Come lie with me, my sister.

12 And she answered him, Nay, my brother, do not force me; for no such thing ought to be done in Israel: do not thou this folly.

13 And I, whither shall I cause my shame to go? and as for thee, thou shalt be as one of the fools in Israel. Now therefore, I pray thee, speak unto the king; for he will not withhold me from thee.

14 Howbeit he would not hearken unto her voice: but, being stronger than she, forced her, and lay with her.

15 Then Amnon hated her exceedingly; so that the hatred wherewith he hated her was greater than the love wherewith he had loved her. And Amnon said unto her, Arise, be gone.

16 And she said unto him, There is no cause: this evil in sending me away is greater than the other that thou didst unto me. But he would not hearken unto her.

17 Then he called his servant that ministered unto him, and said, Put now this woman out from me, and bolt the door after her.

18 And she had a garment of divers colours upon her: for with such robes were the king's daughters that were virgins apparelled. Then his servant brought her out, and bolted the door after her.

19 And Tamar put ashes on her head, and rent her garment of divers colours that was on her, and laid her hand on her head, and went on crying.

Some persons of ill motives (or at least persons who are un-taught) never say a single "word" out of what is proper. However, there are other dangerous games that people play – some people practice making sensual sounds as if they were placing an obscene phone call – but you say "I didn't say one single word". True enough; but you are not respecting your date by leaning over in your date's ear and making sounds like an obscene phone call.

Now, some of you might be saying that Holiness.com is just being ultra legalistic – you might be thinking that these guidelines are not relevant for the real world. Well, let me tell you something: in the secular world, among people who do not necessarily profess to know God – sexual harassment training has become standard curriculum for staff among companies large and small. For example, sexual harassment prevention training that I was required to attend in a secular company for which I worked warned individuals of even looking (glancing) at others in a manner that might be interpreted as a sexual advance. For more proof of the inappropriateness of certain looks see Isaiah 3:16: "Moreover the Lord saith, Because the daughters of Zion are haughty, and walk with stretched forth necks and wanton eyes, walking and mincing as they go, and making a tinkling with their feet." These "wanton eyes" are said to refer to lusty, flirtatious glances made with the eyes (without even saying a word or making a sound). Or, Proverbs 6:25 says: "Lust not after her beauty in thine heart; neither let her take thee with her eyelids." It appears, that possibly this woman communicates an entire paragraph of seduction without uttering a single sound.

Continuing with this discussion of non-verbal communication, let me say that there should be no reason to show your date a pimple on your thigh (your date is most likely not a practicing dermatologist anyway).

There should be no reason to show your date that mole on your chest.

Let me stress something that many of you don't fully comprehend:

There is a difference between men and women. You might think this is quite obvious, but many people don't seem to understand the difference. For example, the passion of a man can quite easily be set ablaze by seeing a beautiful woman in skimpy clothes – even a woman that is a total stranger. While this type of strong reaction will erupt in some women, it is even more pronounced in men, and will exhibit itself even in the average man. This is why lewd and wicked magazines and movies are such a lucrative business.

Thus, there is no reason for you to show your date that mole on your chest.

VIRTUOUS APPEARANCE

Since there is a lot of confusion in the church-world today regarding how Christians should present themselves in public, let me give you some guidance on modesty of appearance/apparel that will go a long way toward helping you present yourself as a virtuous Christian.

As a Christian, you don't want the reputation of being wild. Some people may have a very tamed personality, but their appearance seems to indicate that they are wild and rebellious. I have seen one gospel singer who would be a very attractive woman – except for the orange hair. Yes, this dear lady has colored her hair orange – similar to the color you would see on "PoPo The Clown". I have also seen men with hair died shocking red. No, I won't say they are going to hell for doing this; going or not going to hell is not the point I am trying to make here. I am trying to help you present yourself in an attractive and godly manner. Ladies and Gentlemen, my advice is for you to stay away from shocking and bizarre hair colors. I think some of the weird and wacky hair colors and hair styles that I am seeing today are the result of people hungry to get attention.

Speaking of hair, please look at the following words from

I Corinthians 11: 14 and 15:

> 14 Doth not even nature itself teach you, that, if a man have long hair, it is a shame unto him?

> 15 But if a woman have long hair, it is a glory to her: for her hair is given her for a covering.

Yes, I understand that sometimes a lady's hair may fall out because of illness, stress, or other unavoidable causes. Nevertheless, a lady should not intentionally cut her hair to resemble a masculine style.

As for the men with long hair that flows down to their shoulders, or hair braided in various feminine styles, know that God created you a man and you should want to look like a man. What sort of frame of mind is a man in when he wants to look feminine?

Ladies, if you are going to wear earrings, don't put so many rings on your ear until you look like a pincushion. Some ladies will wear 10 earrings at once. Anything, even a good thing, can be so overdone to the point of overindulgence.

Gentlemen, I recommend that you don't wear earrings. You don't want someone to confuse you with a pirate, player/gigolo, pimp, gangster or homosexual.

Sometimes, when a person is saved off of the streets of a rough and tough community, there may be a tendency to bring the standards of conduct and dress from the bar, alley, or red-light district over into the church. Things such as face mutilation (e.g., piercing the eyelids, lips, and tongue with sharp objects) are not the symbols of modesty. Certain restaurants will not even allow you to work as a server and display these face mutilations because they recognize these to be offensive practices. Do I need to tell you that a chicken bone (or sharp stick) worn/punctured through the soft tissue of your nose is not the symbol of a modest Christian?

Tattoos? I recommend that you just say "No!" to getting tattoos. Much of the things that I mention above simply have pagan undertones, in addition to being immodest. There are demonic rituals that exist even today where people mutilate themselves to show courage, or devotion to their gods. Besides these reasons, I am told that there are sexual undertones to getting one's tongue pierced – I will not go into what the undertones are said to mean.

If you want to shock someone, shock them by being modest and pure in your heart and in your appearance. I was once at an amusement park with my family when my eye caught a group of youth who were all so modestly and nicely dressed. I found this so curious that I got close enough to find out what group they were affiliated with. My point is that their modesty was actually an eye-catcher; not weird and bizarre things such as spiked hair (hair shaped into large pointed spikes with the sides of the head shaved bald).

Now, I am sure that some of you want to know where I stand on the subject of makeup/cosmetics. Let me first give you a piece of scripture. I Timothy 2:9 "In like manner also, that women adorn themselves in modest apparel, with shamefacedness and sobriety; not with broided hair, or gold, or pearls, or costly array;" It seems to me that Paul is stressing that the Christian should not let the wearing of jewels and costly merchandise become so excessive as to be gaudy and conspicuous. An example of this might be a friend of mine who used to wear at least one fancy ring on every finger and many metal bracelets.

For those of you who believe that this scripture is saying that a Christian should never wear gold or jewelry, I would ask that you send all your gold and jewels as a gift to me that I might sell them and use the proceeds for godly purposes.

Does God really mean for everyone to give away his or her gold wedding ring? I don't think so, because the Bible makes references to the wearing of rings as a natural and acceptable thing. In Jesus' parable of the prodigal son, we see the father putting a ring on his son: "But the father said to his servants, Bring forth the best robe, and put it on him; and put a ring on his hand, and shoes on his feet." (Luke 15:22)

And, another passage in the second chapter of the book of James makes specific reference to the wearing of gold:

> 1 My brethren, have not the faith of our Lord Jesus Christ, the Lord of glory, with respect of persons.
>
> 2 For if there come unto your assembly a man with a gold ring, in goodly apparel, and there come in also a poor man in vile raiment;
>
> 3 And ye have respect to him that weareth the gay clothing, and say unto him, Sit thou here in a good place; and say to the poor, Stand thou there, or sit here under my footstool:
>
> 4 Are ye not then partial in yourselves, and are become judges of evil thoughts?
>
> 5 Hearken, my beloved brethren, Hath not God chosen the poor of this world rich in faith, and heirs of the kingdom which he hath promised to them that love him?
>
> 6 But ye have despised the poor...

If you believe that God is always consistent, then you must believe that God's Word (the Bible) is consistent. In my mind, to reconcile I Timothy 2:9 with other passages in scripture where godly people are wearing jewelry, rings and costly (or goodly) apparel, I must conclude that Paul is referring to the inappropriateness of Christians wearing costly items to the point of being conspicuous – i.e., rings on all 10 fingers. I believe Paul may also be focusing on the extraordinary amount of time and money that some devote to styling their hair. Some people get hair styles that literally take many hours and multiple days to complete which cost $100 (US dollars), $200, or more. Some of these same people will cringe with emotional pain if asked to sit in a worship service more than 60 minutes, or if asked to contribute $40 dollars to a Christian mission that feeds the hungry.

No, I cannot say that you are wrong for spending $200 dollars on your hair, or for spending all day at the beauty salon. However, I will say that if $200 dollars is too much to give in the church offering plate, or if spending all day at a church service or a religious seminar is totally unacceptable to you, then maybe spending this kind of time and money on your hair is too much for you, personally.

Some of you may be wondering what the word "shamefacedness" in I Timothy 2:9 means. Well, to be "shamefaced" is to exhibit extreme modesty and moderation. I have looked at the Greek from which the word "shamefacedness" originates. This Greek word, *aidos*, intimates a woman who is discreet and conservative in the way she displays herself in the presence of men.

Contrary to this scripture, many of the church ladies today look as if they have just been initiated into a savage tribe of bloodthirsty warriors. Instead of going on a date, they look as if they are about to go on the warpath. They have eyelids painted with all sorts of exotic colors. They have bold colored paint plastered across their cheeks. Their lips look as if they have either been drinking blood, or kissed the side of a freshly-painted barn before the red paint has had time to dry. They have fingernails that look like the talons (claws) of some great winged dragon, except that these talons are painted with an assortment of unnatural colors with gemstones glued on. These ferocious, frightening looking ladies do not bear the image of "shamefacedness". Many of them actually claim to be a holy prophetess of God.

Whatever powders, creams or potions and notions you use should only serve to give you a natural look; ideally, men should not recognize that you have makeup on – it should look just as natural as when they make-up the President to do a campaign speech on TV. Oops, you mean you didn't know that they makeup the president for his TV appearances? Sorry to burst your bubble. But, this is exactly my point: you are supposed to look as if you don't have makeup on, if you choose to use it. You are not supposed to paint your face so as to attract attention. Remember the word "shamefacedness"?

Woe unto everyone one of you who sells products designed to keep the man's gaze locked on the enticing woman who lacks shamefacedness. The false concept that a woman must look brazen and seductive, is rooted in the lie that a woman must walk around looking like pure sexual passion in order to attract a man. This lie seems to ignore the many virtues and great worth of a godly woman. God did not make the woman to be a sexual object enslaved to the tactics of enticing men through sensual stratagems.

Dear friend, break off those bands of slavery and exploitation and know that if a man has to be seduced into being interested in you, he is not worthy of you anyway. But, you say: "I don't feel that I have been enslaved". In American history (the 19th century) when the slaves were freed by proclamation of the government, there were some slaves who continued for some time under the hardship of slavery – they simply did not know that they had been freed. Upon hearing that slavery had been abolished, at least a few slaves doubted whether they should leave the plantation – they had been deceived into thinking that there was no other life they could live. But, many, many slaves knew that slavery was not right; they knew that they deserved a better life; they desired to be treated with the respect that their God-given dignity deserved.

You may ask, "but how do I know if I have been exploited?" Well, my sister, know for sure that you have been exploited if you have GDLP – Greazy, Dripping Lips Syndrome. You may have never heard of GDLP because I made up the term. However, you may have seen GDLP all around you. GDLP is this stuff that I see the ladies wearing on their lips that makes it look as if they have smeared hot, melted hog-fat on their mouth. I guess the object is to give their lips a glossy, dripping-wet shine. I ask you the question: "Why are you using a product to make your lips glimmer and shimmer with a wet, honey-dripping effect?" Are these products not advertised to make your lips tantalizing and irresistible?

Look, I don't want anything that is going to drive a woman (whom I am not married to) wild with passion. I really must question your motives of trying to use your lips to ignite the passion of some man you are not married to. Don't be naïve; thoroughly study the marketing techniques used to sell products, such as the one you are using. Just look at how the commercials portray the use of these products, and you may be forced to agree that the primary intent of the product you are using is to give a sensual look.

Is it not an unnecessary bondage to have to carry around these applications of bright luminous colors, which the enslaved individual must purchase and apply to her lips many times each day? Dear Sister, your lips are already beautiful enough; save your money and self respect. If your lips are a little chaffed – just purchase some lip balm at the corner pharmacy. Leave the bright lip applications for PoPo The Clown.

Should I list the many colors the enslaved sister must purchase because the world tells her she is not beautiful unless she paints her eyelids various colors (green, blue, purple, silver, gold, and etc.)? I cited Proverbs 6:25 earlier. I will now show you the larger context of that verse, because I believe that it is relevant to our discussion:

> 20 My son, keep thy father's commandment, and forsake not the law of thy mother:
>
> 21 Bind them continually upon thine heart, and tie them about thy neck.
>
> 22 When thou goest, it shall lead thee; when thou sleepest, it shall keep thee; and when thou awakest, it shall talk with thee.
>
> 23 For the commandment is a lamp; and the law is light; and reproofs of instruction are the way of life:
>
> 24 To keep thee from the evil woman, from the flattery of the tongue of a strange woman.
>
> 25 Lust not after her beauty in thine heart; neither let her take thee with her eyelids.
>
> 26 For by means of a whorish woman a man is brought to a piece of bread: and the adulteress will hunt for the precious life.

God does not change the passionate nature of a person who becomes a Christian. Thus, a considerate and wise Christian takes steps not to arouse the passion of a brother or sister to the point where it is difficult for the brother or sister to keep from sinning.

Let me return to the subject of appropriate attire. Men, there is no need for you to have your shirt open down to your navel. As a matter of fact, there is no good reason at all for you to show your chest in public (unless your clothes catch on fire and you have to rip your shirt off in a hurry).

Ladies, your clothes should not reveal any portion of your breasts. You should not even show cleavage. And, those backless dresses are just not suitable for a Christian lady; if the back of your blouse is cut below your shoulder level (or worse yet, the dress is sleeveless), don't buy that dress.

It has become the fashion fad even among church folk to wear shirts so small as to show one's navel. Ladies and Gentlemen, buy the proper size for your height and weight, and don't show your belly in public. If your shirt or blouse is too short to fully cover the middle section of your body (back, front and both sides), donate that shirt or blouse to some young child in need of clothes.

And, let me say that I am so insulted by men intentionally getting pants with waistlines much larger than their waists, so that their pants drop down and they show their undershorts (or worse yet, show their *Gluteus Maximus*).

Some weeks ago, my niece was helping me prepare to sell Holiness.com products at a gospel concert, where she was offended by seeing a young man with his pants dropped so low that he was showing the cleavage of his backside.

My comment to my niece was this:

> That is why we [Holiness people] draw a line as far as appropriate attire. Because, if we don't draw a line, people will show the line [of their *Gluteus Maximus*].

I hope that I do not need to tell you that women should not be showing their *Gluteus Maximus* either.

If you own one of those cleavage showing, back-exposed, sleeveless getups, and you just can't bring yourself to throw it away, save it for your wedding night in the privacy of your hotel room (with just you and your husband); we shouldn't see you in such attire in the public. Again, you say that Holiness.com is just being legalistic; you say that clothes don't matter. Turn to Proverbs 7:10: "And, behold, there met him a woman with the attire of an harlot…". "Harlot" is the old English term for a prostitute; is that really the look you want? Is that the impression you want to give your date? (Just in case you are wondering how it is I know what a prostitute looks like, let me tell you that one of the jobs that I have held was in law enforcement.)

Regardless of race or age, the officers that I had to ride along with could identify who was a prostitute within seconds, based primarily on a lady's dress and mannerisms. I read in a "Christian" magazine a gospel singer's defense of dressing provocatively. Basically, the singer claimed to be attempting to identify with the type of people that needed to be reached with the gospel. I believe in identifying to a certain extent. Nevertheless, if I am witnessing to a male stripper or male prostitute, I don't need to dress just like him to reach him. By the way, when I see how some of these church men are attired on their way to go swimming, they look like strippers.

It was somewhat embarrassing to me, when I was approached by friends originally born outside of the USA who were interested in my opinion as to why many Americans dress so scantily in public. I really cannot justify dressing in a provocative way. I simply have told my friends that modesty is still right.

It seems like everywhere I turn (on television, on magazine covers at the grocery checkout counter, even in the church), people are promoting the concept that a woman must attract a man by immodestly exposing her body. What type of man will you attract by dressing up like a harlot? At some "Christian" gatherings, the church folk are exposing so much flesh that it looks like a meat market.

It is entirely possible for one to look nice (even fashionable) in their clothing without looking unholy. One of the key things here, is not to look sensual (i.e., sexy). Men, those tight shirts and pants you intentionally bought too small when you used to go out dancing (before accepting Christ) – throw those away. Ladies, you can throw away those skin-tight clothes you owned, as well. It is simply not enough to be fully covered, if your clothes are so tight (and/or see-through) that your clothes reveal EVERYTHING.

Don't let the latest fashion pressure you into wearing that skimpy outfit that exposes your thighs. You may wonder: "How far down should my garment cover?" Here's a really safe rule that will almost guarantee your garment is long enough:

> Get in the privacy of your bathroom, in front of a full-length mirror. Stand up; then sit down (normally as you always sit); walk around. If your knees show while performing this demonstration, then the garment may be too short. Try another garment.

Again, the garment that is long enough should still not fit so tightly that your clothes look like a second skin. I once read of someone with clothes so tight that the person's carotid artery was cut off. Some use the excuse that they gained weight since they bought the outfit. Well, either let the seam out, or buy some bigger clothes until you lose enough weight to fit that outfit properly.

And, let me also say that it does not do any good for you to have a garment that is long enough, but has a split so high that you still show your thighs.

The sad thing is that thousands, maybe even millions of women, willingly participate and profit directly from the women who have enslaved themselves to the use of sensual tactics. How so? - every one of you who sells products designed to keep the man's gaze locked on the sensuality of the immodest woman. If you sell products to other women as part of some firm, please don't push the products that make your customer look like a seducer, even if that is the product that will gain you the most profit, or get you to the "next level" of your marketing organization. You may make less money, but how about pushing those products that only serve to enhance the image of purity and beauty within your customers? Your firm may not give you the big bonus, but you will have preserved your integrity and God will be glorified. Do you remember I Timothy 6: 10? "For the love of money is the root of all evil: which while some coveted after, they have erred from the faith, and pierced themselves through with many sorrows."

Don't get me wrong; I am not trying to say one should be ashamed of his or her body. You miss my intent altogether if that is your reading of this guideline. The book of Psalms confirms indeed that you are "...fearfully and wonderfully made..." (see Psalms 139: 14). You, my Sister and my Brother, are wondrous and beautiful creations of God. Even the physical part of your being, your body, is an exquisite and amazing work of art.

I am not suggesting that Christian men and women must walk around wearing large burlap sacks the size of piano covers. I am not saying that we have to be covered from the crown of our heads to the feet with only a peephole to see through, as with garments such as the bur'qa. (The bur'qa is the garment that resembles a large blanket that covers the entire head and body, which women in certain Islamic sects have been required to wear.) I believe that it is nice for women to look feminine and for men to look masculine, each exemplifying the grace and beauty unique to his or her gender.

Don't worry, my Brother and my Sister; if you properly adorn yourself, your date will still see clearly enough that you are attractive, even beautiful. Yes! It is not a sin that you find your date so beautiful that you are strongly attracted to him or her. However, the full secrets of your beauty, my Brother and my Sister, are not to be revealed except within the intimate bond of marriage. What I am trying to get across is that there is supposed to be a limit on what your dates see of your person. There should be a preserving/hiding of your nakedness until you are legally married to that one you love. Marital intimacy is like a treasure to be shared between husband and wife, not between girlfriend and boyfriend, not even between two persons engaged to be married.

For those of you who enjoy eating pastry desserts, I want you to imagine that you have just stepped into a bakery. In this bakery there are all sorts of delicious desserts carefully placed behind the counter or in the refrigerator (for those things that must be kept cool). Now, imagine on one table near the entrance doorway of the bakery, that there is a cake. This cake is for all the potential customers to pinch off a piece to sample/taste. As potential customers come in to the bakery they handle, breathe on, pinch, poke and sample the cake. Even a stray fly or two lands on the cake. Now it is the end of the day, and you step into the bakery, and the baker tries to get you to take the remaining portion of the cake home with you, free of charge. I would imagine, unless you are really, really hungry, that you would decline the offer. You would probably rather pay money to get one of the cakes from the refrigerator that has been carefully protected from being handled, even breathed on, by people passing through the bakery.

In the same way, if you display yourself in the public by revealing and exposing yourself, or if you conduct yourself sensually in front of persons you are not married to, many prospective spouses may not want to take you home to meet their family (and rightly so, because you look like you are willing to be "handled, breathed on, pinched and poked" by every passerby – do you understand what I mean?).

Even if you could convince the world that you are not a promiscuous person, conducting yourself in a sensuous manner entices people of the opposite sex to sin.

Again, let me say that men must take care to be properly, modestly clothed, even if all of the women in their immediate circle are neither enticed to sin nor offended by their immodesty. I once had a school friend who tried to convince me of the merits of nudist beaches by saying that the people on a particular nudist beach in another country he went to were not "hung up" (did not care) about people walking around in public without their clothes.

What my friend needed to understand is that Holiness (the way of life that God requires) is not something that we can abandon, based on what groups of people on a beach decide to do. If you are "itching" to walk around improperly clothed, go into your private bedroom, strip your clothes off and have a ball with just you (or you and your spouse, if you are married). But, as for the public, we should not see you unless you are clothed in a manner that reflects the modesty that we should adhere to in public.

Sometimes a person who is not a Christian may accumulate thousands of dollars in clothing and accessories that reflect sensual, worldly standards. When this person becomes a Christian, the question becomes: "Should I really stop wearing these things that reflect sensual, worldly standards?"

Is God your heavenly father, and is He pure and holy? Even if you were a wild and crazy sinner, as a Christian, you should strive to reflect God's Holiness. Behave purely, even dress purely. Yes, Holiness (Christian living) should permeate (soak through) every aspect of your life. God commands all of his people to live according to Holiness (again, Hebrews 12:14 applies to you as well as me). If you say that God Almighty is your father, yet your appearance more closely resembles the god of this world (Satan – see II Corinthians 4:4), you confuse the public as to who really is your spiritual father. And, if you are confusing the public, you are no doubt scaring away potential dates who mistake you for an infidel (nonbeliever).

Imagine, if you would, that you love desserts (cakes, cookies, pies, and etc.) that are made from processed sugar. But, let's say that you are on a strict, doctor-prescribed diet and special medication in preparation for some medical procedure that is extremely important that you have done. Your doctor advises you not to eat anything with processed sugar prior to the operation, or you will die. However, the doctor promises you that if you stay on the diet until after the medical procedure, you will later be able to eat all those lovely desserts that you like.

Well, you have a "friend" who loves desserts just as you do. And this friend is well aware of your diet, and the consequences if you don't follow the diet. However, this friend invites you over for a visit. When you arrive at your friend's home, the friend invites you to sit on the couch which has a coffee table in front of it that is covered with candy dishes with all sorts of chocolates and sweets (made from processed sugar). Your friend then steps away into the kitchen to put something into the oven. You feel yourself becoming tempted to pinch a little piece of chocolate, so you move to a seat at the dining room table. But, on the table in front of you are dessert magazines laid open to recipes to some of your favorite desserts. In the mean time, your friend returns to the room and you chat about current affairs in each other's lives. You gradually become more and more distracted by the fragrant, sweet, and aromatic smell of carrot cake. You abruptly tell your friend that you have to leave and quickly walk, almost running, to the door to escape the home of your "friend."

In this parable, regardless of whether your friend had ill motives or not, regardless of whether your friend was aware of his or her actions, your friend was doing things that were enticing you to do something that might kill you. Was your friend forcibly making you eat dessert? The answer is "no". However, your natural strong desire to consume desserts was being ignited and intensified greatly by the sights and smells of your friend's home. It is somewhat like a person who instigates a riot and then later says that he or she was not guilty of rioting because he or she never threw a punch or broke a window. Both those who threw punches, broke windows, as well as instigated the riot, will end up in jail.

In our parable you were right to run out of your "friend's" home and save your life. There is just no good reason for one to present himself or herself to the public in a seductive manner. Whatever the reason for doing so, you are a threat to the spiritual life (and maybe physical life as well) of those around you.

DATE LOCATIONS

While we're on the subject of maintaining one's purity while dating, let me say something about the location of a date.

We have, in today's world, church folk who do such things as take their dates (alone) on a 3-day cruise to Mexico. I have nothing against cruises to Mexico – I took my wife on one and had a marvelous time. However, how in the world are Christians to not only maintain purity, but exemplify a model of circumspect living to the world, if we are taking overnight trips alone with our date?

There are too many good places to go on dates without going off alone with your date to some island resort. It is not good to fly down the coast for a weekend alone. I don't care if you have already purchased your tickets to Paris for both of you – take the tickets back! If you feel like you have to violate sound principles to hold on to your date, maybe you should look elsewhere for a date. Or, maybe you are not yet ready for the dating scene until you have developed further in the way of Holiness.

Even if you don't leave town, it is not good to lounge around together at your date's home with no other adult there but the two of you. To make matters even worse, you have some singles that will hang around their date's apartment until all hours of the night. What does that look like, when you slip out of a woman's (or man's) apartment at 2:00 AM in the morning? But, you say: "We were so enraptured with talking about the glory of the Lord." Well, God is still good, even if you talk about him on the phone rather than the wee hours of the night alone in some apartment with someone you are romantically attracted to.

Now, let me give you another tip: even if there is another adult in the house besides you and your date, don't take your date off to some dark back room (or basement) to entertain. You say the acoustics are better when you watch TV in the dark? I don't know all about the impact of dark on the sound from a TV speaker, but I do know that people do feel more comfortable "making their move" on their date while they're sitting together in the dark. I recommend that you wait till you're married to sit in the dark leaning on one another, watching TV.

To the men, I say that as much as 50% of the time (or maybe more) a woman is not to be trusted as having right motives who tries to convince you to go overnight somewhere on a date, or tries to get you to take her somewhere way off and remote (for example, hiking in the forest, camping alone), or tries to get you off in some secluded situation (e.g., dinner at her apartment, ALONE, or parked in some abandoned, remote location).

You ask: "Well, what about the other 50%, or less, of these women, who suggest such ideas and who don't have ill motives?" I say to you men, the other 50% of the time, don't trust yourself. In case you have trouble doing the math, 50% + 50% means just don't put yourself in these situations at all. You may think this is out-dated and too old-fashioned, but I ache and hurt in my spirit to see so many dear people in this age of information and knowledge still falling into sin, or unknowingly walking into dangerous situations that end up affecting their lives in very painful ways. These guidelines will help prevent you from placing yourself in some of these hurtful situations.

In my imagination, I hear someone saying right now that they "know someone who violated all these guidelines and never sinned nor gave anyone the impression that something improper was going on". Well, I must respond by sharing this true story:

> Once, while a young lad in the mountains during winter, I happened on a stream that had frozen over solid, where we could walk back and forth across the top of the stream. However, during one of my crossings, I stepped onto a portion of the stream that was not fully frozen (it was somewhat slushy – ice and water mixed). It seems as though I sunk down into the ice-cold of the stream up to my chest never touching the bottom of that deep stream with my feet. Before I was pulled downstream under the sections of the stream that were covered by solid hard ice, I was yanked from the stream in a mild state of shock.

Now, I survived this ordeal without any physical injury. But, I would be remiss in encouraging you to walk on thin ice because I did it without any resulting physical injury. And, I would be less than godly if I told you to ignore due prudence when dating, just because I know someone who did not behave wisely and survived the dating scene without any notable negative consequences.

PHYSICAL DANGER

To the Ladies, I ask (I PLEAD and BEG) you not to trust a man enough to go on overnight trips. Please! Please, don't go off to remote or secluded locations, even in the light of day. There are just too many wicked men in the world to even risk being trapped in a vulnerable situation. Even if you believe that an evil man could not physically overpower you, I would rather you try your best not to be in a situation were an evil individual would think he could get away with trying to assault you. Even if a brother is a walking Bible (as far as quoting scriptures) and speaks in multiple unknown tongues, don't go to secluded places because even Paul witnessed that there are sometimes phonies among the Christians; in II Corinthians 11: 26 Paul said that he was in danger "among false brethren".

I hate to say this, but you have some men who may play the organ for the worship service on Sunday mornings as they look out on the audience lusting after women, scoping for victims. Some churches so desperate for skilled musicians overlook the fact that their organist is a known lecher.

A number of years ago, I was standing in the main corridor of the hotel lobby at a Christian conference. I believe I might have been helping someone from our party carry packages. In any case, there was a gentleman in the hallway whom I did not know, who appeared to be with the convention as well. Somehow we struck up a very brief (maybe 5 minute) conversation, in which he informed me that he was a member of a local church; he even told me his Pastor's name. Well, I thought I had met another good Christian brother. To my surprise, this gentleman took it upon himself to figure out how to contact me by phone at my hotel room. I tried not to be rude, but was getting a bad feeling about the man, especially since he did not seem to have anything to say or any real purpose in calling me at my hotel room. This man's next move was to try and convince me that he needed to meet me in my hotel room. Well, the conclusion was that I told him very plainly and firmly that anything he needed to discuss, he should talk it over with his Pastor. What I would like you to take from this incident that happened to me is that some really bad people sometimes come to church conventions for ill motives. For that matter, they sometimes attend local churches, Christian colleges, seminaries, gospel concerts, church dinners, gospel skate parties, and you name it. Please don't be paranoid, but do be prayerful, wise and watchful.

This area makes me so angry concerning those wicked predators who attack innocent ladies. Physical assault is never acceptable. No matter how much your date paid for dinner, no matter how much your date has done to impress you with an enjoyable date, your date never has the right to assault you. If someone has taken advantage of you in this way, I recommend that you seek the counsel of your Pastor, or other like responsible authority figure. It might also be advisable to get ongoing counseling in a Christian based treatment program for those of you who have been the victim of traumatic situations as described in this section. Also, it is not un-Christian to report these wicked criminals to the authorities. Romans 13:1-5 says:

> 1 Let every soul be subject unto the higher powers. For there is no power but of God: the powers that be are ordained of God.
>
> 2 Whosoever therefore resisteth the power, resisteth the ordinance of God: and they that resist shall receive to themselves damnation.
>
> 3 For rulers are not a terror to good works, but to the evil. Wilt thou then not be afraid of the power? do that which is good, and thou shalt have praise of the same:
>
> 4 For he is the minister of God to thee for good. But if thou do that which is evil, be afraid; for he beareth not the sword in vain: for he is the minister of God, a revenger to execute wrath upon him that doeth evil.
>
> 5 Wherefore ye must needs be subject, not only for wrath,

but also for conscience sake.

The bottom line is that the passage above is letting us know that the Government is authorized by God to distribute damnation (judgment) to wicked criminals such as rapists, and God will also judge them. Can a rapist be converted to Christianity? Of course. Yet, the rapist may still have to serve the full sentence of the judgment determined for the crime of rape.

You cannot be a Christian and a practicing rapist; the two are diametrically opposed to each other. So, if you have any tendencies toward such wicked criminal activity, or assault of any kind, get help (professional Christian help). Again, to those who may have been attacked, seek counsel as stated above, with regards to reporting the crime perpetrated against you. Even if the civil authorities are unwilling to act, God gives church fellowships the power to ban wicked individuals from their midst who pose as Christians. I Corinthians 5:5 "To deliver such an one unto Satan for the destruction of the flesh, that the spirit may be saved in the day of the Lord Jesus."

Ladies and Gentlemen, if you even hear someone speaking about wanting to sexually assault someone, be sure to make it plain to that individual that there is no acceptable reason for this kind of activity, that it is a wicked deed, and that it is a crime to commit such an act against someone. Depending upon how you feel God is leading, you may need to direct this individual to psychological and spiritual counseling.

Given that there are all sorts of people that may cross your path, there is a fact that you need to understand about the ego (whether you consider yourself inexperienced or experienced, wise or foolish, young or old). Your ego (e.g., pride) can sometimes cause you to act in a manner that is dangerous. God may allow the person who is behaving wisely to sometimes fall into dangerous situations. On the other hand, the dangerous situations we find ourselves in are sometimes due to our unwise actions. There are some occasions where people ignore the wise Biblical teaching of their mentors and place themselves in dangerous situations that could have been avoided. I am definitely not trying to say you are the blame for the actions of some man, or woman that has treated you abusively on your date. The thing that I am trying to encourage you to do is to be as shrewd and discriminating as you can be when dating. I want to show many of the pitfalls that are prevalent in dating so that you might avoid at least the obvious dangers.

Let me clarify what I am saying a bit more: The ego (of both men and women) makes you think you can go anywhere and handle any situation in your own power, by your own smarts and ability – nothing could be further from the truth! Men and women have been caught, enticed or sometimes physically forced to do things they definitely did not want to do. I personally know someone that was taken advantage of through the use of drugs. This person knowingly accepted something known to be a mind-altering substance. But, the person did not know that these "friends" this person was hanging out with ultimately intended to abuse this person after this person used the mind-altering substance.

Even men have allowed themselves to be taken advantage of in the most horrible ways through allowing themselves to become intoxicated. Let me pause here and say that I teach strictly against drinking alcoholic beverages or any other intoxicating/mind-altering recreational substances.

Take a look at Proverbs 23:19-35:

> 19 Hear thou, my son, and be wise, and guide thine heart in the way.
>
> 20 Be not among winebibbers; among riotous eaters of flesh:

21 For the drunkard and the glutton shall come to poverty: and drowsiness shall clothe a man with rags.

22 Hearken unto thy father that begat thee, and despise not thy mother when she is old.

23 Buy the truth, and sell it not; also wisdom, and instruction, and understanding.

24 The father of the righteous shall greatly rejoice: and he that begetteth a wise child shall have joy of him.

25 Thy father and thy mother shall be glad, and she that bare thee shall rejoice.

26 My son, give me thine heart, and let thine eyes observe my ways.

27 For a whore is a deep ditch; and a strange woman is a narrow pit.

28 She also lieth in wait as for a prey, and increaseth the transgressors among men.

29 Who hath woe? who hath sorrow? who hath contentions? who hath babbling? who hath wounds without cause? who hath redness of eyes?

30 They that tarry long at the wine; they that go to seek mixed wine.

31 Look not thou upon the wine when it is red, when it giveth his colour in the cup, when it moveth itself aright.

32 At the last it biteth like a serpent, and stingeth like an adder.

33 Thine eyes shall behold strange women, and thine heart shall utter perverse things.

34 Yea, thou shalt be as he that lieth down in the midst of the sea, or as he that lieth upon the top of a mast.

35 They have stricken me, shalt thou say, and I was not sick; they have beaten me, and I felt it not: when shall I awake? I will seek it yet again.

Let us provide you with The Living Bible (TLB) rendering of this passage:

19, 20, 21 O my son, be wise and stay in God's paths; don't carouse with drunkards and gluttons, for they are on their way to poverty. And remember that too much sleep clothes a man with rags.

22 Listen to your father's advice and don't despise an old mother's experience.

23 Get the facts at any price, and hold on tightly to all the good sense you can get.

24, 25 The father of a godly man has cause for joy – what pleasure a wise son is! So give your parents joy!

26, 27, 28 O my son, trust my advice – stay away from prostitutes. For a prostitute is a deep and narrow grave. Like a robber, she waits for her victims as one after another become unfaithful to their wives.

29, 30 Whose heart is filled with anguish and sorrow? Who is always fighting and quarreling? Who is the man with bloodshot eyes and many wounds? It is the one who spends long hours in the taverns, trying out new mixtures.

31 Don't let the sparkle and the smooth taste of strong wine

deceive you.

32 For in the end it bites like a poisonous serpent; it stings like an adder

33 You will see hallucinations and have delirium tremens, and you will say foolish, silly things that would embarrass you no end when sober.

34 You will stagger like a sailor tossed at sea, clinging to a swaying mast.

35 And afterwards you will say, "I didn't even know it when they beat me up…. Let's go and have another drink!"

Countless marriages have been destroyed as a result of individuals consuming alcoholic beverages.

In my country of residence, thousands upon thousands have died as the result of someone drinking alcohol and driving.

It has been observed that often alcohol is involved when crimes (even murder) are committed.

I ask you this: "Why would you invite recreational mind-altering substances (i.e. dope) into your life?"

These substances weaken your resistance to temptations of sin. Is that what you want?

ACCOUNTABILITY

There are all sorts of freedoms that one can experience in society today. As a young person comes to the legal age of adulthood, the young person is given more freedom to make his or her own decisions. Even in the scriptures we find the Bible speaks of freedom or Liberty that belongs to Christians. But, you need to know that freedom, or independence, does not mean independence from responsibility. It does not mean independence from accountability. Maybe you have just reached the age where you have gained the privilege of going on dates. Do you think because you have just reached the age of dating, that you can go anywhere, with whomever you want, anytime you want, without letting those you are accountable to know about your general whereabouts? If this is what you think, don't go on one single date until you totally digest this entire book (and understand the guidelines that are contained in it).

I was watching the news channel some time ago and the program I was watching related the most horrible story. There were a couple of young ladies (in their teen years) who took a trip to the shopping mall. While at the shopping mall, these young ladies met a couple of guys who seemed to be interested in the young ladies. These men seemed to be real nice older guys – I believe they were in their twenties or thirties. The young ladies were apparently flattered by the attention they received from these "nice" "gentlemen".

These young ladies eventually left the shopping mall and all seemed well, until one of the young ladies decided to slip out of the family home one night to see the suave (smooth) man she had only just met at the mall. I imagine the attention this older man gave to this young lady made her feel mature and grown-up, possibly it flattered her ego. Maybe she felt that the rules and restraints placed on her by her mother were unreasonable for a young lady her age. Maybe she felt justified in slipping out the bedroom window in the middle of the night.

Maybe this young lady felt she could handle any situation she got herself into. Or, maybe she felt nothing could happen as long as other people were there at the man's apartment. I don't know whether the man convinced her he was having a house party or what, but when the man got her into the apartment, he trapped her in a room, and abused her in the most awful manner. And, aided by wicked criminals, began his brutal methods to force the young lady into prostitution.

After some passage of time, the young lady eventually escaped from this situation. Yet, I don't know how long the scars of this awful event will haunt this poor, unfortunate young lady.

My message here is not just for young ladies; young men should also give account to the others living in their household as to their comings and goings.

And, not only those that are young teenagers, but those who are much older need to demonstrate a level of accountability. It is foolish for an adult to come and go from the home, with those who occupy the home never having the slightest notion of where you are and who you are with. You stay out all night, and show up at home at 3:00 AM, and nobody has had the slightest clue as to where you have been. This type of behavior reminds me of when I used to work in law enforcement. It is a sad thing when you have to file a missing persons report for a family member living in the house with you, and you don't even know where the person was supposed to be because he or she comes and goes like a stray cat.

Do I give account? Yes! Even though I am married with a family, I will give my wife at least a general description of where I am during the day. Most days I am at work and she can either reach me directly or leave a message for me. Even on the weekends, if I decide to leave the house unexpectedly while she is gone, I will leave a memo. Now, you don't have to communicate exactly as we do in our home, but there must be some person(s) you have some level of accountability to if you are a Christian, unless you are a castaway on a deserted island.

And, don't feel you can control anything and anyone, or any situation because you are on your turf. Don't feel like it is okay to go on a date with Mike the Maniac, or Susie the Seductress because you are taking them in *your* car and you feel you can keep anything bad from happening. By all means, take your car on the date, but still don't date someone who is living an ungodly life.

As you make use of the advice given above for avoiding dangerous situations, I also suggest that individuals going on dates use technology (i.e., cell phones) to assist in being able to end a bad date, even men may want to have a cell phone (e.g., if the lady refuses to be civil and it's her car – he also might need to get out of the car and find another way home). Technology is still no excuse for taking chances on date locations. If you find yourself in a tempting or dangerous situation, call somebody on your cell phone for support and help. Don't let your ego fool you into thinking you can handle things when you cannot.

PERSONAL REFERENCES

It is good, if at all possible, to have personal references on the person you are starting to date. Too often we have people who blow into town from nowhere with a tall tale (a lie) about who they are. These con-artists become whatever it is they think will best win themselves into your heart. If you want someone that loves children, they make themselves out to be a schoolteacher. If you want someone who is mission-minded, they have a story of how they were a missionary in some far-away land. If you seem to be sympathetic toward those who are downtrodden by society, then this person has a super-sad, tear-jerking story to push your sympathy button.

When you have a personal reference for the person that is interested in dating you, then it may help to more quickly differentiate the good prospective dates from the bad ones.

Let me demonstrate what I mean:

When I met my wife, I was 3,000 miles from home, visiting some friends that I had in her area. If she had told me that she was a brain surgeon, her supposed occupation would likely have come up in my conversation with my friends who knew my wife. And, if she was really a professional gambler, it would have been fairly easy to determine that she was lying to me by talking with my friends. If you have a mentor, friend, or relative who is discreet (not a blabber mouth), who knows the person who is interested in dating you, it is no sin to ask your friend what the reputation is of the person who is interested in you. As a matter of fact, it was one of my friends that actually introduced me to my wife. And, at least one or two of my other friends indicated to me that my wife was an honorable person.

"A good name is rather to be chosen than great riches," (Proverbs 22: 1a) Whether my wife was rich or poor did not matter to me. It was her good reputation that helped increase my interest in her.

Be aware that some people may actually investigate your background in order to fabricate stories about themselves intended to make you think you both have lots of common interests (e.g., you both desire to do missionary work in Central America). While you are believing that you have a match made in heaven, it may simply be that he or she has done some Private Investigation work on you and your personal history, and has fabricated a phony autobiography that matches yours.

Have you ever heard couples say: "Oh my date and I are perfect for each other. We like all of the same things. In fact, we are just alike." Now, it could be that one person in this couple is not being honest about his or her likes and dislikes. Or, it may be that in the early days of dating, you have not had enough time to explore the personality of your date to find that you are not "exactly alike". If you are truly "exactly alike," then maybe one of you is redundant.

It is definitely okay to be different from your date – e.g., you may have a variety of things you like, that your date dislikes. The key is whether those differences involve things that will cause irreconcilable conflict. Let me make the following parable:

> Jane could never be happy being married to a Pastor, and her date, Bill, knows for a fact that God has just called him to start/Pastor a church. These two may never get beyond having simply a platonic relationship.

When I say "platonic", I am speaking about a relationship where there is not a desire to pursue a romantic interest. And, let me say that there is nothing wrong with having friends of the opposite gender. I believe that I said before that dating can result in finding some good friends. When two Christians date and later find such differences as I describe above, I find it quite natural for them to become friends, if while dating they have treated each other in a respectful and holy manner.

Maybe you really like the idea of getting a reference on a person and you would like to utilize the information that can be obtained from talking with references. Perhaps you feel that you will not be able to utilize the idea of references for someone you have begun dating because you don't have any friends or relatives who know your date well enough to provide reference information. A reference from someone who does not really know your date is generally not useful. In any case you don't want gossip (made-up stories) or totally biased information concerning your date. You want reliable information.

Aha! But don't give up too soon on the idea of getting reference information. Is your church affiliated in any way with the church of your date? Is your date's church in your same town? Or, is your Pastor acquainted with your date's Pastor? In some situations, it is appropriate to have your Pastor or church official (e.g., youth Pastor) contact your date's Pastor. Do this only if you and your Pastor feel it is appropriate for your situation and the protocol of your culture. If you have a Pastor who will hold your information confidential, he is the ideal person to do this for you, as it is natural for him to have concern for your well-being and to take an interest in whether you are dating a good person or not.

Oh, by the way, I am presuming that you have a good reputation. Be aware that it is only fair for your date's Pastor to inquire concerning your character.

Again you don't want gossip about the person, but you want a general reference on the person's character and maybe some confirmation that the individual is not a dangerous person.

Following are some examples of questions that your Pastor might be able to tactfully get answered for you (you replace the "X" with the name of your date):

Is X a member in good standing (e.g., X meets the minimum requirement to maintain membership at his or her church)?

How long has X been a Christian?

How long has X been a member?

Is X faithful to prayer, Bible study and worship services?

Is X free/eligible to date?

Remember, these are only examples of questions. Generally

speaking, how much information it is appropriate to ask for may be dependent upon how well your Pastor knows your date's Pastor. In any case, how your date's Pastor answers each question (the tone of his voice) may be just as important as the words he answers.

You may feel as though you can always tell if someone has good motives or not, simply by looking at a person's physical features. Here, I am speaking of the physical features that you are born with (e.g., the shape of one's nose). Be most careful with this line of reasoning, because physical features are more a matter of heredity. Large eyes, or small, beady eyes may tell you nothing of a person's character.

Often, people can be physically attractive and extremely talented, and still be undesirable as a prospective date.

Let me give you an example, unrelated to dating, that still makes my point concerning the point of using references. There was a Christian organization that I assisted on occasion. The head of this organization made a decision to offer an individual a key role in the organization without adequately assessing the gentleman's background. I made an inquiry to a friend who was very well acquainted with the individual. My friend was so vague in how he answered my questions, that I picked up right away that the individual we were discussing was not even a Christian. My friend finally broke down and revealed information that gave the individual the appearance of being a con-artist. Needless to say, the organization soon suffered at the hands of this individual's unlawful behavior.

But don't even let good references cause you to give unrestrained trust to the person you are dating. A person may receive a high rating from your friend, but that is only one piece of the puzzle.

I am not saying that you should date only people that are from your circle of friends. However, I am saying that you should do things to validate the history of the person interested in dating you. Not only validate the history, but you quickly need to understand the social circle this person comes from. I am sorry if I sound like a private investigator. I am not suggesting that you tie your prospective date to a chair and perform a military-style interrogation. You must use finesse in obtaining information about the person interested in dating you. And, it may take time to build a minimal picture of who your date really is.

In the meantime, until you build a relationship that is built on certifiable facts, why not take a Christian couple you know well on your dates? Yeah, Yeah, I know you may feel that double dates are not hip and cool. But, remember that thing about accountability we discussed above? What is it that you will be doing or discussing on a date with some person you don't even know well, which requires that you must be alone?

A big date is coming up with that person you don't know well, and there are absolutely no responsible Christian couples at your church (or in your social circle) available the night of your date, to double date with you? Well, there is no harm in taking your sister along. Yes, your sister. You don't have a sister? Well, how about someone who has played a sisterly role to you.

Or, why not meet this person whom you don't know well at the location of the date? You drive your car there and he or she drives his or her car there. If, when you arrive at the location of your date, you find it to be a roadside motel, just keep on driving. Find a well-lit and safe location to call your date and verify you have the correct address. If you had the right address, then I think maybe you would be better off canceling the date.

Believe it or not, it is all too common an occurrence where "Religious People" attend the worship service at a Christian convention only to later swap hotel room keys with single (and married) individuals that they are pursuing ungodly relationships with.

Another tip I would like to give you is that you have one of your mentors meet someone you are dating, well before your heart strings become so tied into the person that you cannot objectively discern whether the person is a good prospective date for you. You see, once your heart becomes tied into a person, there is a tendency to see only the positive things about your date. Even the negative things that you know about your date, you justify.

For example:

> Despite the fact that your date loves to hang out with friends and drink alcohol, you rationalize that your date never gets really drunk; you even use the Bible to defend your date's behavior by arguing that some Biblical characters drank juices that had become fermented.

However, it is possible that your mentor might have been able to provide some objective feedback to you regarding your date, and possibly convince you to forego dating someone who loves alcohol.

I am trying to give you some wise suggestions here. You may be able to come up with a few more ways to help you discern good prospective dates from bad ones. But, hopefully, you will seriously consider the suggestions I have provided above.

Will you have to turn down some dates, or at least postpone them because they would require you to put yourself in an uncomfortable situation? Yes! You may have to turn down some dates. Some of you may think that what I just said is sacrilegious. But, listen to me, if you are so hungry for a date that you are willing to throw all caution to the wind, you have the wrong attitude about dating.

I truly understand the natural desire a person has to be significant, special, etc., in the eyes of at least one other person. Where we run into trouble is when we are willing to do that which is bad to have people show us special attention, and to have people (of the opposite sex) to desire to be around us. If a person's desire to be around you is based upon your crossing the boundaries of godly pre-marital behavior, then you do not need the attention of that person. If you must practice sexual seduction by means of sensual teasing and enticement to gain someone's attention, then you do not need the attention of that person because such sexual seduction and manipulation is not right.

You and your date may feel that you are in control of the situation and that your sensual behavior is only in fun. You may feel that you are in total control of the situation and that nothing "really bad" will happen. I have not always been a Christian. And I tell you that sin can be like poison; some poisons, you can take a little at a time and your demise is so gradual that you do not realize that you are dying. If you continually and gradually lower your standard of doing unwise things on dates, you may not realize that you are going further and further down the path to destruction.

It's kind of like a former gambler who just likes to hang out at the casino for enjoyment. He or she may say that they would never gamble again. But, if he or she always loiters around the gambling table, sooner or later, he or she will find himself or herself sitting at the table asking the dealer to deal him or her a hand of cards.

If you never start down the path of bad choices, you have much less worry about becoming entrapped in sin.

Some people convince themselves that they will try bad decisions, and if it causes them to sin, then only at that time will they concede that they cannot handle the activity that led them to sin. They don't realize that the more you sin, the easier it may become to sin again.

The second time is easier than the first, the third time becomes easier, and the fourth time is even easier. At some point, the Holy Spirit may even stop convicting you of what you are doing. For example, look at the act of smoking marijuana, or drinking alcohol – the more a person drinks alcohol, the more the person may be able to drink in larger quantities, until his or her body, mind, soul and personal relationships are destroyed.

THINGS TO DO ON A DATE

As I said before, there are so many great places to go on a date. Places that are much less likely to place you in a vulnerable situation:

> You can go to a restaurant; if that's too expensive, there is nothing wrong with going out for ice cream at the local ice cream shop (whether you're 19 or 119 years old); for the physically fit, rollerblading, or skating in the park; there are even gospel concerts that are sometimes absolutely free of charge, for the more economical budget; I am not ashamed to say that I still enjoy going to the zoo – it can be just the right place; or, maybe encourage your church to organize a trip to that popular amusement park; sometimes family events such as picnics can be a good place to invite a date; miniature golf, anyone? Get creative; how about shopping – maybe Christmas shopping together?

Although I would love to go more often to luxuriant places with my wife, the problem with many of us in Western civilization is that we feel we must always spend huge amounts of money in order to have a fantastic time. Really, the more important thing is "who you are with", not "how much money you can squander" on a particular date. Having said this, I do believe those of you who may be more blessed financially/materially, should not feel embarrassed or restricted from going on dates that sometimes cost more than the average person can afford. It might be ridiculous for me to suggest that you millionaires must always restrict your dates to the cost of a hamburger, fries, and milkshake. Nevertheless, if you have a date that is always pressuring you to spend beyond what your income is, I caution you to evaluate the character of the person you have chosen to date.

I once recall when I was a young student before accepting Christ, that a young female friend of mine insisted that I take her to dinner. I plainly told her that I did not have the financial resources to do so. She insisted so vehemently, that I agreed to go if we could both pay our own way. Well, the evening of the date arrived. After receiving the meals that we ordered, my date seemed to suffer selective amnesia and could not remember that she was paying for her own meal. Well, the result was that she did pay for hers as I only had enough money on my person to pay for my meal. Curiously enough, we never went out on a date again, although we did remain friends.

If someone invites you on a date and says that the date is "Dutch," or "Dutch treat", the individual expects you to pay your expenses during the date. (However, I suggest that one might consider using terms other than "Dutch" or "Dutch treat" to describe this kind of dating. I suggest this as I am uncertain how people of Dutch heritage feel about the name of their people group being associated with dating practices that might be viewed as ungenerous.)

The natural question comes up: "Who really should spring for (pay for) the date?" This might seem like a simple question, but it can be a little more difficult than it first appears. My personal recommendation is that it is usually good for the man to attempt to pay for more of the dates than the lady. Before I explain why I make this statement, allow me to say that there are certain acts of chivalrous behavior that really seem to be rooted in Biblical principles. Specifically, I believe that the nature in which a man will lead his family is sometimes demonstrated by whether he always relies totally on the lady to finance their dates, or whether he feels the greater responsibility to finance the majority of their dates. This is not to say that the lady should never finance the date. And, this is not to say that the lady should never pay her own part/half of the date. In some cases, until a lady has known the gentleman for a while, and is sure that the man is not the kind to think he can disrespect a woman whom he treats to dinner, it may be best for the lady to pay her own way.

Nevertheless, a man who does not feel the greater responsibility to finance the dates may possibly also feel that he does not carry the financial responsibility to care for his wife and children when he becomes married.

If we look at many of the examples of the married individuals in the Bible, we see these male patriarchs gainfully employed in trying to meet the financial/material needs of their household. We see these patriarchs leading out in the home in this way, even when their wives are employed in various gainful and industrious endeavors. Even those men such as the Apostle Peter, who appears to have let his fishing business fall by the wayside, still seems to have had a concern for the material sustenance of his household, even as he labored most vigorously and resolutely as a fisher of men. See what the Apostle Paul says in I Corinthians 9:4-11:

> Have we not power to eat and to drink? Have we not power to lead about a sister, a wife, as well as other apostles, and as the brethren of the Lord, and Cephas[Peter]? Or I only and Barnabas, have not we power to forbear working? Who goeth a warfare any time at his own charges? Who planteth a vineyard, and eateth not of the fruit thereof? or who feedeth a flock, and eateth not of the milk of the flock? Say I these things as a man? or saith not the law the same also? For it is written in the law of Moses, Thou shalt not muzzle the mouth of the ox that treadeth out the corn. Doth God take care for

oxen? Or saith he it altogether for our sakes? For our sakes, no doubt, this is written: that he that ploweth should plow in hope; and that he that thresheth in hope should be partaker of his hope. If we have sown unto you spiritual things, is it a great thing if we shall reap your carnal things?

So, even men employed in the full-time ministry, who rightly receive materially/financially from the body of Christ, use the "fruit" and the "milk of the flock" to assist in providing for the sustenance of their household.

Thus, unless there are some extremely extenuating circumstances, I tend to be uncomfortable as a rule with a gentleman who relies 100% upon the lady to finance all their dates. Here, in America, we have too many "party guys" who are healthy, strapping individuals (i.e., in no wise disabled) who are content to run the streets all night, sleep late in the morning, hang out with the "fellas" (fellows) in the afternoon, and allow their poor little wife to support them. Even if a man is independently wealthy, he needs to be involved in some noble effort (e.g., building housing for the homeless, feeding the poor, spreading the gospel through tract distribution, and so on).

Well, you ask: "What if the man is poor and the lady is rich? And, what if the lady is not satisfied with going on inexpensive dates when she is perfectly able (and willing) to personally bear the cost of expensive dates?" If the man and lady agree that they will expend larger sums of money on their dates than the poor gentleman can afford, and if they agree that the lady will bear the financial burden for these expensive dates, I will not make a general statement that this is always unadvisable. However, I would recommend poor brothers dating financially well-off sisters to consider whether he is really emotionally secure enough not to become intimidated, jealous, or bitter toward the lady because of her financial success. Furthermore, if this dating relationship continues, I think that it is imperative that this couple seriously consider and work through how the role of each person might be manifested if they were to eventually marry. For example, exactly how will this financially-independent woman affirm her husband's role as her head, given the fact that 99.9% of everything they will have together, she will have brought to the marriage?

I am not saying that this couple should not date (or eventually marry); I am saying there are some unique questions that must be resolved given that many men and women I know would be very much challenged to achieve the Biblical model of a wife and husband (who is the head) within the financial circumstances that I describe above.

No matter how much you are attracted to your date, don't let your love (or infatuation) for your date cause you to violate what is reasonable. I give you these guidelines for your protection, not because I am trying to spoil your fun. I speak to you this brotherly advice as those who spoke to me as mother and father figures when I was entering into the dating scene and progressing through it.

THE DANGER OF BEING IMPATIENT

I must stress the point that if you have an uncontrollable, passionate infatuation for a person, yet you have no respect or appreciation for who that person really is inside, then you are not in love with that person. Worse yet, you may have no more regard for that person than a man would have for his mistress, or a one-night-stand.

A relationship built solely on a physical, sexual attraction will end up being a horrible mess. It is fine to date someone that you are attracted to, but don't take it for granted that a person is the man (or woman) of your dreams only because you like the exterior of the package.

Believe me when I say that I understand the loneliness that you may feel as a single person. I was single quite some time before getting married. Despite your feeling that God is not moving quickly enough, please don't compromise these guidelines, because the mess you make by rushing ahead of God may cause you years of heartache.

You that are single may see the romance and affection enjoyed by married couples all around you. You may become frustrated with your attempts to find a mate. But, have patience. Don't get ahead of God and wrongly try to duplicate marital passion and intimacy outside of marriage – this is not God's will.

How can you expect to carry on a relationship in a sinful, ungodly manner and expect God to make it blossom into a beautiful, lifelong, godly relationship?

The manner of your behavior (what you sow) will determine what happens in the future (what you reap). Galatians 6:7 and 8 says the following:

> 7 Be not deceived; God is not mocked: for whatsoever a man soweth, that shall he also reap.
>
> 8 For he that soweth to his flesh shall of the flesh reap corruption; but he that soweth to the Spirit shall of the Spirit reap life everlasting.

I know of cases where individuals simply got tired of waiting and decided to take matters into their own hands and rush into marriage with someone other than the Christian that God wanted them to be with. I must admit that I came too, too close to marrying someone who just wasn't God's will for me to marry. Fortunately, God was faithful to lead (drag) me out of that situation. It took a few proverbial whacks on the head for me to realize that God had other plans for me.

If you are attracted to someone who is not saved from sin, don't you save that person so that you can "legitimately" date them. If you saved someone, he or she is not saved. What I mean by you "saving them" is that you pressure him or her to say he or she is a Christian when the person has no intention of living for God. Or, you naively and falsely imagine him or her to be a Christian, when the evidence of his or her actions shows that he or she is still under the control of sin. A person becomes a Christian by turning from his or her sins and turning to Jesus. Every Christian, by definition, has faith in Christ to the degree that he or she is willing to learn and follow the teachings of the Bible. What I am trying to stress is that many times it is quite clear that your date is not truly a Christian in action and deed. And, a person who lives a life that is opposite to the Bible is not a Christian. Now, some of you may be offended at my making such bold statements, but before you close your mind to what I am saying, let us look at the Bible; James 2:14-19 says:

> 14 What doth it profit, my brethren, though a man say he hath faith, and have not works? can faith save him?
>
> 15 If a brother or sister be naked, and destitute of daily food,
>
> 16 And one of you say unto them, Depart in peace, be ye warmed and filled; notwithstanding ye give them not those things which are needful to the body; what doth it profit?
>
> 17 Even so faith, if it hath not works, is dead, being alone.
> 18 Yea, a man may say, Thou hast faith, and I have works: shew me thy faith without thy works, and I will shew thee my faith by my works.
> 19 Thou believest that there is one God; thou doest well:

the devils also believe, and tremble.

20 But wilt thou know, O vain man, that faith without works is dead?

Let us look at this same passage in The Living Bible (TLB) as well:

14 Dear brothers, what's the use of saying that you have faith and are Christians if you aren't proving it by helping others? Will that kind of faith save anyone?

15 If you have a friend who is in need of food and clothing,

16 and you say to him, "Well, good-bye and God bless you; stay warm and eat hearty," and then don't give him clothes or food, what good does that do?

17 So you see, it isn't enough just to have faith. You must also do good to prove that you have it. Faith that doesn't show itself by good works is no faith at all – it is dead and useless.

18 But someone may well argue, "You say the way to God is by faith alone, plus nothing; well, I say that good works are important too, for without good works you can't prove whether you have faith or not; but anyone can see that I have faith by the way I act."

19 Are there still some among you who hold that "only believing" Is enough? Believing in one God? Well, remember that the demons believe this too – so strongly that they tremble in terror!

20 Fool! When will you ever learn that "believing" is useless without doing what God wants you to? Faith that does not result in good deeds is not real faith.

Now, it is possible that someone you find to be attractive has sincerely and honestly repented. Maybe this person visited your church, and while there, became convicted of his or her sins. Maybe he or she came to the altar, and while there, asked Christ to come into his or her heart and forgive his or her sins. Don't be in such a hurry, that you are asking for a date before the person can walk from the altar back to the pew he or she was sitting in.

And if you are one of those notorious matchmakers on a mission to pair up every single person who walks in the door of the church, be aware that a person may (or may not) meet a prospective spouse at his or her local church. The primary purpose of the Church is not to pick up dates. I tend to think that some people become meddlesome matchmakers because they are bored with their own dating experiences (or spouse, if married). You show a lack of wisdom if a brother or sister just came to Christ this morning and you are ready to marry him or her as quickly as you can get a marriage license.

It might be better for you to allow a person who has just repented a little time to show the evidence that he or she has repented.

Matthew 3:7 and 8:

> 7 But when he saw many of the Pharisees and Sadducees come to his baptism, he said unto them, O generation of vipers, who hath warned you to flee from the wrath to come?
> 8 Bring forth therefore fruits meet for repentance:

The Living Bible (TLB) renders these two verses as follows:
> 7 But when he saw many Pharisees and Sadducees

coming to be baptized, he denounced them. "You sons of snakes!" he warned. "Who said that you could escape the coming wrath of God?

8 Before being baptized, prove that you have turned from sin by doing worthy deeds.

BEWARE! WHEN YOUR DATE SAYS:

Do you remember what was said earlier, concerning consideration of your date:

> If you truly esteem/value your date, the date's Christian relationship with God will be greatly regarded: this great regard should be apparent by your conscious effort not to do or say things that would tend to tempt your date to do anything that would be displeasing to God.

It is sometimes difficult to understand why God has let sin exist in the world. God, in his divine wisdom, allows Satan and sin to continue in the world at this point in history. Yet, God intends for us to behave wisely in order to defeat temptations. To this end, I will expose some tactics below that have caused individuals to fall into sin. I expose these that you might recognize and oppose them when they are being used, and thereby maintain your holy integrity.

Trust me when I tell you that there are individuals who may attempt to take advantage of your attraction to them. These individuals may try to manipulate you to do things that will lead you into sin and away from God.

BEWARE! WHEN YOUR DATE SAYS:

- "If you really like me, then why don't you trust me to go on a weekend trip alone";

- or, there's the stale and overused: "If you really love me, you will prove it by…"; in too many cases the things that these folk want you to do to prove your love places you at risk of physical harm or temptation to sin, or both;

- or, how about the big lie: "We can go anywhere and do anything that married people do, because marriage is just a piece of paper anyway; we have true love in our hearts for each other and that is a more important commitment than going through a legalistic, stuffy ceremony to get married";

- or, there's the very creative deception: "The way I feel about you, I am already married to you in my heart, so it is okay for us to…";

- or, the false cliché: "We are both saved, mature people, 'Two clean sheets can't dirty each other'" – Maybe I need help on what people mean by this one. If people mean to say that it is acceptable for two Christians to fornicate together, then this is a huge lie;

- or, some might say: "Just try it, just this once, and if it doesn't work for you, then I won't ever bring it up again";

-or, your date might say: "We don't have to really do **it**; we can just stop short of doing anything that you feel is uncomfortable for you";

The path into bondage and sin is sometimes a gradual and subtle one. Satan's tactic is often to gradually tempt/move a Christian in the direction he wants you to go, and then when you are out on a limb, he saws the limb off. If something is wrong, don't even let yourself be led halfway down the path toward wrong – not even 1/10 of the way down the path of wrong.

- and, there's the date who has something that they need to talk to you about, but they can't talk with you about it unless you are willing to go off to some deserted or remote location. DANGER! You may be excited, and prone not to exercise good judgment, thinking that you are going to get a marriage proposal; unfortunately, too many have received less noble propositions in these secluded locations than just an innocent marriage proposal.

- or, there's the: "Since we are engaged and plan to get married, it's okay for us to…" Look, the standard for physical conjugal relations is marriage, NOT ENGAGEMENT! Don't you know people who have been engaged prior to finding the person that they actually married? Well, I know Christians who were engaged and the wedding was called off for one reason or another (and was never rescheduled).

- or, how about the old guilt routine: "I would do anything for you, I guess you just don't feel the same way about me".

By the way, some of these people will even shed tears in the midst of their theatrical, manipulative show. Some people in our local community are as gifted at conjuring up displays of emotion as any actor or actress. The real issue is not the fervency of emotion, or display of sincerity, but the end result of what you are being asked to do.

- or, how about Adolescent Routine #1 (sometimes used against someone with a juvenile mind): "Hey, all my friends are doing it, everybody is doing it." – whatever "it" may be for your date. I can almost hear my mother saying now: "If everybody jumps off the Golden Gate Bridge, are you going to do it too? If all your friends eat mud and drink swamp water, will you do it too?"

- and, there's Adolescent Routine #2: "I know someone who did it, and nothing bad came of the experience, so you don't have to be afraid."

I once had the opportunity to visit what we in the USA call the Grand Canyon. As I stood at the top of the cliff, I looked across to the opposite side of the canyon some distance away (the canyon is reported to be 18 miles wide in some places). I then moved over to the observation deck of the cliff and looked down into the canyon toward the Colorado River, which ran through the bottom of the Canyon, one mile straight down below where I stood. A traveling companion who stood next to me on this observation deck, located on the edge of the cliff, seemed un-impressed by the magnitude of the height at which we stood. He seemed to sense no danger, and began leaning over the safety rail that stood between us and a one-mile drop down to the Colorado river. Oh, did I mention that he had been smoking dope (Marijuana) prior to leaning fearlessly over the protective railing? No, he did not fall over the side of the cliff; so, I guess you can say that nothing happened because of his action. So, is it okay to advocate smoking dope and leaning over a cliff? However, if you were to hear the testimony of this gentleman today (he later accepted Christ), he would tell you of the painful consequences he still suffers as a result of the wild life that he led years ago. What I am getting at is this: you can ignore these guidelines if you wish, but eventually the consequences will catch up with you.

- has your date tried to manipulate your ego/machismo? Some very unwise people will risk their very lives performing foolish stunts, rather than endure someone thinking that they are not daring or brave. Do you remember as a child calling someone "chicken" or a "scaredy cat" in order to goad them into doing something risky? Unfortunately, this tactic is used successfully against some individuals who ought to be old enough to do what is wise and right, despite having their bravery challenged by their unwise and/or immoral date.

- a twist on the ego/machismo theme is this: "Aw, you're just scared your mommy is gonna catch you and give you a spanking" or "You're letting that preacher and those church folk control your mind". "I tell you what, I know a special place we can go where no one knows either of us; nobody will ever know that we were there." I guess you are then supposed to agree to sneak off secretly; or, you are supposed to flex your ego and say: "I am my own person, I will go if I want to, and I don't have to sneak around when I go."

- as I have stated before, some individuals feel that they are under some special dispensation that gives them a right to act immorally. One preacher that I heard about felt that he had achieved some level of spirituality that allowed him to be lewd. What I am told is that this preacher made an improper physical advance on a young lady. The young lady being godly, was greatly offended and retorted to the preacher: "How could you do such a thing?" His response was simply: "I PRAY HARD."

- a reversal strategy involves those who suggest an improper activity or location for a date (as described previously), who challenge your stature in Christ if you reject their suggestions as being improper. They say: "if you were prayerful enough, like me, you would be spiritual enough to handle going with me to the…" I wonder if these individuals think that they are greater than Jesus. Jesus, full of the Holy Ghost (Luke 4:1) fasted forty days. Satan was allowed to throw temptations at Jesus as recorded in the fourth chapter of the book of Luke. I want you to look at verses 9 through 12 of Luke, chapter 4:

"And he brought him to Jerusalem, and set him on a pinnacle

of the temple, and said unto him, If thou be the Son of God, cast thyself down from hence: For it is written, He shall give his angels charge over thee, to keep thee: And in their hands they shall bear thee up, lest at any time thou dash thy foot against a stone. And Jesus answering said unto him, 'It is said, Thou shalt not tempt the Lord thy God'."

Simply put, we are not to play the game of foolishly placing ourselves in danger to prove how spiritual, or strong in Christ we are – that is an egotistical and extremely dangerous game. This game reminds me of a church that I saw on television were the worshipers danced and shouted as they held live poisonous snakes and drank from jars containing poison – the best I can recollect of this television program, the truly faithful believers were supposedly saved from getting hurt because of their great faith, or spirituality, or some such similar reasoning.

- and, for the "ultra, super spiritual" con artist, he or she just wants to: "come over to your apartment so we can study the scriptures together, alone." Or, "Can you meet me at my apartment? I just feel that we can get a better breakthrough, spiritually speaking, if we pray alone together." You better believe someone may indeed end up as prey (i.e., victim).

Even if I am to assume that your "ultra, super spiritual" friend is indeed a Christian, I must at least caution you that this person may be immature, or a Christian who is untaught. We sometimes become so awe-struck and impressed just because someone mentions prayer and Bible reading and quotes a few scriptures. It is really prayer and Bible reading exemplified by a Christ-like life in daily situations that should impress us. Don't be duped by a fake show of godliness. Sometimes, the best test of godliness is what a person does when he or she is not aware others are watching. If you feel that you know the person well enough, and it would not violate the customs of your culture, why not consider popping in unexpectedly to the prayer meeting or Bible study service at the church your date attends. If you find that he or she is never there, or is never on time on the occasions that you pop in without prior notice, then you should question whether you are dating someone who truly does not hold prayer and the Bible in high regard.

> - or, there's the lie: "God does not understand you like I do; it's just too hard and not fair for you to deprive yourself of the fun of going alone with me to… or doing…" Hebrews 4:15-16 says:

Seeing then that we have a great high priest, that is passed into the heavens, Jesus the Son of God, let us hold fast our profession. For we have not an high priest which cannot be touched with the feeling of our infirmities; but was in all points tempted like as we are, yet without sin. Let us therefore come boldly unto the throne of grace, that we may obtain mercy, and find grace to help in time of need.

> - Fake right, Run left: sometimes, what seems to be an excellent date scenario/plan, turns out to be a cover for your date's "real" plans to get you into a romantic situation or in a secluded situation. For example, your date's mother doesn't show for dinner at the home that the three of you were supposed to have dinner at. When you recommend postponing the dinner until a time when Mama is available, your date says "Don't be a stick in the mud" and suggests the two of you continue with your plans without Mama. Well, I want to encourage you to be a "stick in the mud". There are variations on this same theme: on the way to Mama's house he or she wants to stop over at his or her apartment and would like for you to come in to show you "something". When you decline to go inside, your date says: "don't be a party pooper". Well, I say: "be a party pooper".

- Even if you were promiscuous in the past, don't let someone who knows your past try to use it against you by bringing up things that you formerly participated in. Don't even give the person a chance to describe what you did in your past, because it will only make you angry, depressed, or tempt you to fall back into those sins. I Corinthians 6:9-11 says:

> Know ye not that the unrighteous shall not inherit the kingdom of God? Be not deceived: neither fornicators, nor idolaters, nor adulterers, nor effeminate, nor abusers of themselves with mankind, nor thieves, nor covetous, nor drunkards, nor revilers, nor extortioners, shall inherit the kingdom of God. And such were some of you: but ye are washed, but ye are sanctified, but ye are justified in the name of the Lord Jesus, and by the Spirit of our God.

God has forgiven you of your past life of sin. Don't go back to that life for any reason.

There is the myth that if a young lady does not plan to fornicate, but it just happens by "accident," then she is more virtuous than the young lady who makes plans to fornicate. Let me help you here: men, women, boys, and girls – none of you need fornicate by "accident", nor on purpose. If you are fornicating (i.e., having sex outside marriage), you are not virtuous. If you are reading this book and rebel against its principles, you have chosen to fornicate. You did not slip into sin; you ignored the road signs and road blocks of Biblical teaching that were placed along the road, and you decided to drive head-first off the cliff.

- For those who have never lived a promiscuous life, the unholy person will try to convince you of taking part in something that is wrong by saying: "You have to experience THINGS for yourself to be able to help/identify with others".

- There is the hurt puppy routine: this is where the person of the opposite sex tries to appeal to your sympathy to try and manipulate you into a compromising situation. The set-up goes something like this: "I am so lonely. You are the only friend that I have. There are some hurts from my past that I need to share with you because no one else seems to understand me like you do." Here, in this example that I have given, your date is not only appealing to your sympathy, but boosting your ego/pride by saying you are the only person in the world that understands. Your date is also appealing to your curiosity to know and hear what "hurts" he or she feels that only you are privileged to hear.

Now, I am not trying to be overly cynical and skeptical. There are valid and righteous instances where people appeal to your sympathetic nature, and they do not have any ill motives.

Here is the test of your date's motives: If after getting you in a sympathetic mood, your date then suggests some activity or going to some location that normally would make you uncomfortable, then follow wisdom and decline to go.

Anyway, how long have you known this person? Why is he or she taking you in as his or her only and closest confidant, when you have only known each other a short time?

- And, there's the "I wanna be sure" line: "I want to marry you, but I just wanna be sure that you and I are romantically compatible; I need to know for sure that you are as passionate as I am."

Well, what does he or she mean by this? I am not sure. So, your best tactic may be to tell the person that you are not certain what he or she means and ask him or her to speak as plainly as they can. If you keep asking them to explain more plainly and he or she comes down to saying that what they expect is for you to give them a pre-marriage, live demonstration of your passion, then you know that your date's motives are evil. As they say on the farm: "If you can get the milk free, why buy the cow?" If your date can get that which should only be given to your spouse, your date may lose interest in marriage. And, if your date is a person of strong integrity, he or she does not want to rob you of that which does not belong to him or her. Some people just have a problem making a commitment for marriage from the "get-go".

I know of a beautiful person who dated someone for 10 years. If you really desire to marry your date, and it's taking a decade of dating for him or her to make up his or her mind whether you are the right one, I have to wonder whether you have been wasting your time with the wrong person.

In any case, one of the best determiners of whether a person will be "romantic" over the long term has a lot to do with personality traits that are observable without doing things that are improper on a date. For example, you have found a date who has demonstrated over a long period of time that they are sensitive to what you say when you are talking; a date who consistently tries to do those "little" things that brighten up your day; a date who now and then thinks up little surprises for you. I can tell you with a fair amount of certainty that this type of person is more likely to be "romantic" during the course of a lifetime of marriage.

Yes, you have some dates that dress ever so seductively (as if to invite people to lust after them); yet, many of these carnal persons pout and act stubborn, grumpy, and petty whenever they do not get their way (or, they may have other extreme deficiencies with regards to the fruit of the Spirit). I can guarantee you, no matter how passionate this person looks, over the period of a lifetime of marriage (unless God works a miracle on this person's personality), you won't have as much romance as you think when the honeymoon has lost all of its honey.

Oops, just in case you don't have the "fruit of the Spirit" passage at your fingertips, you can find it in Galatians 5:22-25; it reads thus:

> But the fruit of the Spirit is love, joy, peace, longsuffering, gentleness, goodness, faith, Meekness, temperance: against such there is no law. And they that are Christ's have crucified the flesh with the affections and lusts. If we live in the Spirit, let us also walk in the Spirit.

So, beware of the person so sensuous before marriage that they are about to explode like a bomb if they cannot satisfy their lust – for you may find that once married for a while, that his or her lusty feelings fizzle and you are left with a dud. He or she may lose that passionate desire for you altogether. I dare say your passionate lover may not really be in love in the first place. True love is more than a passionate feeling anyway, and true love can last a dozen lifetimes, not just a dozen weeks of pre-marriage fantasy and daydreams.

Is it possible that a person who looks and acts in a sensuous and seductive manner does so unknowingly? Yes, it is possible that these people behave immodestly without realizing the effect of their actions. Yet, if they do so unknowingly, you must wonder what other deficiencies exist in their knowledge. They may have even worse behavioral practices that they perform because they don't know that they are not good.

I tend to believe that many (if not most) individuals who behave sensuously are demonstrating outwardly that the works of the flesh have gained a foothold in their spirit.

What are the works of the flesh?

The Apostle Paul describes the works of the flesh in Galatians 5: 19-25:

> 19 Now the works of the flesh are manifest, which are these; Adultery, fornication, uncleanness, lasciviousness,
>
> 20 Idolatry, witchcraft, hatred, variance, emulations, wrath, strife, seditions, heresies,
>
> 21 Envyings, murders, drunkenness, revellings, and such like: of the which I tell you before, as I have also told you in time past, that they which do such things shall not inherit the kingdom of God.
>
> 22 But the fruit of the Spirit is love, joy, peace, longsuffering, gentleness, goodness, faith,
>
> 23 Meekness, temperance: against such there is no law.
>
> 24 And they that are Christ's have crucified the flesh with the affections and lusts.
>
> 25 If we live in the Spirit, let us also walk in the Spirit.

This passage is also provided in The Living Bible (TLB) below:

> 19 But when you follow your own wrong inclinations your lives will produce these evil results: impure thoughts, eagerness for lustful pleasure,
>
> 20 idolatry, spiritism (that is, encouraging the activity of demons), hatred and fighting, jealousy and anger, constant effort to get the best for yourself, complaints and criticisms, the feeling that everyone else is wrong except those in your own little group – and there will be wrong

doctrine,

21 envy, murder, drunkenness, wild parties, and all that
sort of thing. Let me tell you again as I have before, that
anyone living that sort of life will not inherit the kingdom
of God.

22 But when the Holy Spirit controls our lives he will
produce this kind of fruit in us: love, joy, peace, patience,
kindness, goodness, faithfulness,

23 gentleness and self-control; and here there is no
conflict with Jewish laws.

24 Those who belong to Christ have nailed their natural
evil desires to his cross and crucified them there.

25 If we are living now by the Holy Spirit's power, let us
follow the Holy Spirit's leading in every part of our lives.

If we behave sensuously in front of someone we are not married to,
then we promote/tempt individuals to sin. And, just because you
marry that person, don't expect his or her sensual behavior will be
confined only to you. If the works of the flesh have taken control of
someone, they are likely to fall into all sorts of sin (even adultery).
You can no more tame a person determined to live sensuously than
you can tame a hurricane. It takes God to convert the person who
lives according to the works of the flesh.

The basis of relationships (even romantic ones) for a Christian is
the love that God generates in his or her heart. A person who is
motivated by the works of the flesh will fall well short of this godly
love.

This love that God generates in a Christian is called charity in

ICorinthians 13:1-8. This passage is provided below.

> 1 Though I speak with the tongues of men and of angels, and have not charity, I am become as sounding brass, or a tinkling cymbal.
>
> 2 And though I have the gift of prophecy, and understand all mysteries, and all knowledge; and though I have all faith, so that I could remove mountains, and have not charity, I am nothing.
>
> 3 And though I bestow all my goods to feed the poor, and though I give my body to be burned, and have not charity, it profiteth me nothing.
>
> 4 Charity suffereth long, and is kind; charity envieth not; charity vaunteth not itself, is not puffed up,
>
> 5 Doth not behave itself unseemly, seeketh not her own, is not easily provoked, thinketh no evil;
>
> 6 Rejoiceth not in iniquity, but rejoiceth in the truth;
>
> 7 Beareth all things, believeth all things, hopeth all things, endureth all things.
>
> 8 Charity never faileth: but whether there be prophecies, they shall fail; whether there be tongues, they shall cease; whether there be knowledge, it shall vanish away.

The Living Bible (TLB) may help you grasp the message of this passage:

> 1 If I had the gift of being able to speak in other languages without learning them, and could speak in every language

there is in all of heaven and earth, but didn't love others, I would only be making noise.

2 If I had the gift of prophecy and knew all about what is going to happen in the future, knew everything about everything, but didn't love others, what good would it do? Even if I had the gift of faith so that I could speak to a mountain and make it move, I would still be worth nothing at all without love.

3 If I gave everything I have to poor people, and if I were burned alive for preaching the Gospel but didn't love others, it would be of no value whatever.

4 Love is very patient and kind, never jealous or envious, never boastful or proud,

5 never haughty or selfish or rude. Love does not demand its own way. It is not irritable or touchy. It does not hold grudges and will hardly even notice when others do it wrong.

6 It is never glad about injustice, but rejoices whenever truth wins out.

7 If you love someone you will be loyal to him no matter what the cost. You will always believe in him, always expect the best of him, and always stand your ground in defending him.

8 All the special gifts and powers from God will someday come to an end, but love goes on forever. Someday prophecy, and speaking in unknown languages, and special knowledge – these gifts will disappear.

Do you see the self-sacrifice, discipline, and caring nature of this godly love (charity)? Does this describe the person whom you have been dating? Hopefully, you can say that this passage describes the characteristics of the person you have been dating. If the person you have been dating looks/acts nothing like this passage, then you need to assess whether you should continue dating that person.

- there is the "carrot and stick" method: if you will be physically intimate with your date, he or she promises to give you the carrot (something you want like a marriage proposal). But, if you will not be physically intimate, he or she will do something you don't like (this is the stick, or punishment). This tactic is the same as saying "I want you to sin against Jesus Christ and disrespect yourself for me because I don't feel like waiting until marriage for physical intimacy."

- or, there is the old salesman routine of: "You don't know what you're missing."

Tempting people with promise of Hidden Experiences, or Secret Pleasures is a tactic that Satan has been using since the Garden of Eden. Satan convinced Eve to disobey God and to eat of the tree of the knowledge of good and evil as described in Genesis 3:5 and 6: "For God doth know that in the day ye eat thereof, then your eyes shall be opened, and ye shall be as gods, knowing good and evil. And when the woman saw that the tree was good for food, and that it was pleasant to the eyes, and a tree to be desired to make one wise, she took of the fruit thereof, and did eat, and gave also unto her husband with her; and he did eat."

Now, if we are honest, we must admit that there is some pleasure to be experienced in some types of sin. However, Satan usually downplays the unpleasant consequences of participating in sinful pleasures. It is best to be like Moses: "Choosing rather to suffer affliction with the people of God, than to enjoy the pleasures of sin for a season;" (Hebrews 11:25). The pleasures of sin may seem the better deal in the short term; however, holy living is always more pleasant in the long term (and, many times, in the short term as well).

Might I recount the story of David? David lusted after Uriah's wife, which led to adultery, which led to premeditated murder. I sincerely doubt if David thought the pleasure of his sin was worth the trouble he reaped (e.g., murder in his own family, civil war); in II Samuel 12:9-12, we see God revealing the consequences of King David's sin through Nathan the prophet:

> 9 Wherefore hast thou despised the commandment of the Lord, to do evil in his sight? thou hast killed Uriah the Hittite with the sword, and hast taken his wife to be thy wife, and hast slain him with the sword of the children of Ammon.

> 10 Now therefore the sword shall never depart from thine house; because thou hast despised me, and hast taken the wife of Uriah the Hittite to be thy wife.

> 11 Thus saith the Lord, Behold, I will raise up evil against thee out of thine own house, and I will take thy wives before thine eyes, and give them unto thy neighbour, and he shall lie with thy wives in the sight of this sun.

> 12 For thou didst it secretly: but I will do this thing before all Israel, and before the sun.

Believe me when I say that I understand the discouragement of feeling that you are missing out on the joys of romance and intimacy. You may feel this discouragement very intensely because the people you know all seem to be either happily married or they all seem to be engaging in improper intimate physical touching (even sexual intercourse) with their date, without negative consequences.

Dear Brothers and Sisters, I challenge you to wait on God, and to do it God's way. Wait until after marriage to be found alone with your beloved in that romantic hotel room.

As a teenager, I once went hunting for jackrabbits with my father and uncles (my apologies to the vegetarians). However, the grown men would not allow me to shoot a shotgun. Oh, how I longed to shoot the gun; I was just itching to get a chance to shoot; I could feel shooting way down in my bones, I was just so sure that I could shoot without causing any danger to any of the men. In any case, the men did not let me shoot. The point was that I did not have a license to shoot/hunt. And, if you are single, you just don't have a license (marriage license) that authorizes you to be alone in a hotel room with your beloved, whether or not anything sinful happens.

Why do I expose all of these phrases that are often used to steer one in the wrong direction? Well, my hope is that when you hear these phrases, you will become keenly alert to the words that follow them. And, being alert, you will critically discern whether you are being asked to do something that violates reasonable guidelines – and, ultimately, that you will resolutely refuse to place yourself in dangerous situations. And, finally, you may need to separate yourself permanently from anyone who persists in urging you to abandon reasonable guidelines.

The key is this: once you have explained why you won't do a certain thing or go a certain place, don't feel compelled that you have to get your date's approval concerning things that you have a strong moral belief that you should refrain from doing. If there is a question, seek the wise advice of someone you trust who has demonstrated a holy life, and whom you personally know to have maintained a consistent dedicated godly life. Please, don't go to someone for advice who does not have a good reputation for living purely. Sometimes, these people will give you very bad advice because they feel they can justify their wrong doings by getting other Christians to live in a raggedy manner.

Remember the words of Proverbs 1:10. It says: "My son, if sinners entice thee, consent thou not." Concerning evil, and evil doers, I would quote Proverbs 1:15, which says "…walk not thou in the way with them; refrain thy foot from their path:".

It is sad to say, but with a really bad date, you may have to use the tactic of Joseph. Genesis 39:7-13 captures the essence of this tactic:

> 7 And it came to pass after these things, that his master's wife cast her eyes upon Joseph; and she said, Lie with me.
>
> 8 But he refused, and said unto his master's wife, Behold, my master wotteth not what is with me in the house, and he hath committed all that he hath to my hand;
>
> 9 There is none greater in this house than I; neither hath he kept back any thing from me but thee, because thou art his wife: how then can I do this great wickedness, and sin against God?
>
> 10 And it came to pass, as she spake to Joseph day by day, that he hearkened not unto her, to lie by her, or to be with her.
>
> 11 And it came to pass about this time, that Joseph went into the house to do his business; and there was none of the men of the house there within.

> 12 And she caught him by his garment, saying, Lie with
> me: and he left his garment in her hand, and fled, and got
> him out.

You may indeed have to run, literally, from a situation, leaving your coat, hat, or shoes. You can always get later whatever you left. And, don't let your date bring them by your apartment; he or she can mail them to you if need be. And don't go to your ex-date's house alone to get them; if you must go get them, take someone with you – you don't need a repeat performance of the situation that caused you to run. If your date seemed somewhat belligerent or vindictive, you may be best just considering that coat as a loss. Your safety is worth more than your pride or the monetary cost of buying another coat.

Not to be redundant, but I must caution you that some people who seem to be people of non-violent natures have shown to have hidden violent tendencies when faced with the prospect of you breaking off any dating relationship with them. So, be careful when getting your coat back, even if your date seems to be non-violent or non-vindictive. Potiphar's lustful wife had no right whatsoever to feel angry concerning Joseph's rejection of her advances toward him; yet, see how her desire of Joseph turned to what seemed like hate in Genesis 39:12-20

> 12 And she caught him by his garment, saying Lie with
> me: and he left his garment in her hand, and fled, and got
> him out.

> 13 And it came to pass, when she saw that he had left his
> garment in her hand, and was fled forth,
> 14 That she called unto the men of her house, and spake
> unto them, saying, See, he hath brought in an Hebrew
> unto us to mock us; he came in unto me to lie with me,
> and I cried with a loud voice:

15 And it came to pass, when he heard that I lifted up my voice and cried, that he left his garment with me, and fled, and got him out.

16 And she laid up his garment by her, until his lord came home.

17 And she spake unto him according to these words, saying, The Hebrew servant, which thou hast brought unto us, came in unto me to mock me:

18 And it came to pass, as I lifted up my voice and cried, that he left his garment with me, and fled out.

19 And it came to pass, when his master heard the words of his wife, which she spake unto him, saying, After this manner did thy servant to me; that his wrath was kindled.

20 And Joseph's master took him, and put him into the prison, a place where the king's prisoners were bound: and he was there in the prison.

Joseph sat in prison due to the unjust actions of Potiphar's wife, as a result of Joseph rightly refusing to have improper relations with the woman. Nevertheless, Joseph still had his integrity. Because he maintained his integrity, God later elevated Joseph to a place of honor second only to the Pharaoh of Egypt.

DATING MULTIPLE PERSONS

As we walk through this DATING SURVIVAL GUIDE, it occurs to me that there are some practices related to dating that some may say are definitely always right or some may say are always definitely wrong. There are some practices that may be right or wrong depending upon the context.

Let us consider the practice of dating more than one person. Let us say, for example, that we have a Christian who is not married and is eligible to go on dates, by our guidelines stated previously. Let us say that this Christian is always chaste in the manner that he or she interacts with his or her date. By dating more than one person, I am referring to such instances as a Christian going on a date with a particular person today and also planning to go on a date with someone else the following week. Can I really say that there is a strong moral/Biblical basis for me to claim that the practice of dating more than one person is always wrong? As of this writing, I am not able to formulate a position where I can say that dating more than one person is ALWAYS a bad idea. I will however, give some cautions that one should take into consideration.

Human beings are emotionally sensitive creatures, especially when dealing with love interests. One suggestion I would make to the individual dating more than one person is that this individual not date multiple persons from the same household. I would also suggest that this individual not date people who are close friends. For example, let us say that we have two blood sisters who are very attracted to the same Christian gentleman. If he dates both these sisters at the same time, my mind tells me that it is likely that there may develop a rivalry between the two sisters that may result in there being animosity between the sisters.

Hopefully, you don't desire to be at the center and the cause of two people fighting over you (no matter how important this makes you feel).

Remember what Romans 12:17 and 18 says:

> 17 Recompense to no man evil for evil. Provide things honest in the sight of all men.

18 If it be possible, as much as lieth in you, live peaceably
with all men.

The verse above lets us know that we should strive not to cause
unnecessary confusion.

I would also say that the gentleman in our parable above should be
careful concerning dating the second sister immediately following
the break-up/end of a dating relationship with the first sister. I am
not saying it would be a sin to do so. I am saying that one should
be very, very careful in doing this, as I can see where this practice
would likely cause animosity between the sisters.

And, of course, the principles and cautions above apply to a lady
dating two men who are blood brothers (or any such close family
member or friend).

Please, those of you who proclaim that it is an awful thing to date
more than one person under any circumstance, should understand
that I am trying not to put forward personal preferences as Biblical
mandates. I must admit that when I was dating my wife, that I chose
not to date any of the other women interested in me at the time. And,
my preference was that my wife did not date anyone else. Yet, I still
cannot think of a basis whereby I can make a doctrinal statement
that someone should never date more than one individual in a given
period of time.

Having said this, those of you who have visited Holiness.com
should understand that Holiness.com reaches many peoples of many
cultures of many nations. Thus, if you live in a culture that will
label you as a bad person if you go to dinner with a different person
than you went with last week, you might possibly want to restrict
yourself to dating one person in a given period of time. Sometimes
you must restrict your liberties/actions based upon the context; it is
important to consider the culture in which you are dating and not

necessarily insist on exercising all your dating liberties.

LET ME MAKE IT CLEAR, THAT MY STATEMENT CONCERNING SOME THINGS BEING RIGHT OR WRONG BASED UPON THEIR CONTEXT APPLIES ONLY TO THOSE THINGS THAT I SPECIFICALLY LABEL AS SUCH (e.g., dating multiple persons). I make this disclaimer to prevent those who would falsely claim that all the teachings in this guide can be deviated from, if one feels the context dictates it.

And, of course, some of my brothers and sisters may live in cultures that don't allow dating at all; in this case, dating multiple persons may not even be an issue of concern.

If you feel compelled that you must go on dates with different individuals, let me give you yet another suggestion that I feel does exemplify the Christian Spirit. My suggestion is as follows:

Make sure someway, somehow, that it is understood by your different dates, that you are not going on dates with either of them exclusively. I am not necessarily suggesting that there is a law written in stone tablets that says you must tell every date that you have that it is your opinion that it is okay to date multiple people. But, to be fair, it should come up someway, somehow with people you plan to go out with on a continued basis. If you don't follow my advice on this point, one of multiple things can happen.

You may develop a great relationship with one of your friends of the opposite gender. After dating this person and developing a special relationship he (or she) may discover from a friend that you have also been dating someone else across town. It may then appear as though you have been hiding your dates with the person across town, and your entire special relationship may dissolve into distrust.

Even if you are the one to tell your special romantic interest that you have been dating another all the months he (or she) thought you were dating him or her exclusively, you may still cause some hurt feelings. Your romantic interest may have incorrectly assumed that you were dating him or her exclusively.

Well, you may be of the persuasion that if my dates are Christians and I am a Christian, they just have to trust me regardless of what mistakes I make. Do you not know that there are different levels of trust that we have for people who are even within the body of Christ? Be honest; do you trust everyone in your church with confidential information about yourself? Or, are there a select few (your Pastor, the ladies' auxiliary president, youth leader, your aunt) in whom you have the utmost confidence that they will not reveal personal, confidential prayer requests that you may have shared with them?

On the matter of Christians doing something to cause another believer to lose confidence in that Christian, let's look at Acts 15: 36-41:

> 36 And some days after Paul said unto Barnabas, Let us go again and visit our brethren in every city where we have preached the word of the Lord, and see how they do.

> 37 And Barnabas determined to take with them John, whose surname was Mark.

> 38 But Paul thought not good to take him with them, who departed from them from Pamphylia, and went not with them to the work.

> 39 And the contention was so sharp between them, that they departed asunder one from the other: and so Barnabas took Mark, and sailed unto Cyprus;

> 40 And Paul chose Silas, and departed, being

recommended by the brethren unto the grace of God.

41 And he went through Syria and Cilicia, confirming the churches.

Let us look at this same passage in The Living Bible (TLB) as well:

36 Several days later Paul suggested to Barnabas that they return again to Turkey, and visit each city where they had preached before, to see how the new converts were getting along.

37 Barnabas agreed, and wanted to take along John Mark.

38 But Paul didn't like that idea at all, since John had deserted them in Pamphylia.

39 Their disagreement over this was so sharp that they separated. Barnabas took Mark with him and sailed for Cyprus,

40, 41 while Paul chose Silas and, with the blessing of the believers, left for Syria and Cilicia, to encourage the churches there.

So, my point stands that you should try to avoid concealing the fact that you are going on dates with other individuals, especially if you don't want to cause your dates to mistrust you.

Now, some individuals may insist that if you desire to take them on dates, that you cannot go on dates with other persons. Given this situation, you may have to make a decision not to date other people, or not to date this individual. Whatever you do, don't agree to date only this person, while secretly planning to date others. Lying displeases God and is never the basis of a good relationship.

Now, let's presume that you are going on dates with multiple persons, and let's imagine that everyone (you and your dates) find this acceptable. I still caution you to use some temperance. What I mean to say, is that it might be intemperate to go on dates with thirty different people in a month. You're likely to need a computer just to keep track of where you are going, with whom, and when. I can see you now, mixing up and forgetting the names of your dates – calling your date by the name of the person you had a date with last night.

If I were single, I would probably not ask a lady on a date who has been on dates with half the gentlemen in town. Sometimes, dating too many individuals can reveal that a person is not selective and discerning.

And, on the other hand, don't assume that someone is dating you exclusively, just because that is what you hope is the case. If you feel like your relationship with someone is at a level of commitment that you should only be going on dates exclusively with each other, find a way to get this expectation out in the open. If you simply assume what your special someone is doing, or how the other person feels, you may be greatly disappointed further down the line. I would say that, especially when you are getting to know someone, you should not be making lots of assumptions concerning what your date feels in his or her head and heart.

As ridiculous as it sounds, we have some ladies who would assume they are close to getting a marriage proposal because some brother asked to ride with them on the Ferris wheel at the amusement park.

Or, imagine a church lady who consents to having a picture taken with a casual acquaintance at a Bible conference attended by thousands, only later to learn that the casual acquaintance is going around saying they are going to be married, as he shows the picture as proof of his claim. Can you understand what an embarrassing situation could result from the misguided gentleman's false fantasy?

Believe me, these kinds of incidences do occur in the church, oftentimes as a result of someone concocting a fantasy of what they would like to be true, without any real factual basis.

Please Sir, don't assume that the lovely church lady you have been dating is madly in love with you, simply based on the way she crinkles her nose when she looks at you. It may be that your cologne is just too overpowering and she is afraid to tell you that you have too much on. However, if it is universally understood by everyone in your particular culture that a woman crinkling her nose at a man is done to communicate romantic love, then maybe you are correct in your assumption as regards that lovely lady in your village.

If you think that your relationship with the person you are dating has developed into something really special, and yet your dating partner has not explicitly stated what his or her feelings are about your relationship, I think it is a fair question to kindly ask your dating partner generally how he or she feels about your relationship. Don't pressure your date to say what you want to hear. But, do have enough of a dialogue that allows you to determine whether your date has (or has not) arrived at the same feelings that you possess for him or her. If your date does not possess the same intensity of feelings as you do concerning the relationship, don't be too hasty in ending the dating relationship too soon. If this person has some attraction to you, they may simply need more time to arrive at the same feelings that you have for them – the seed of love does not grow at the same pace in all individuals, as we are all unique beings.

However, let me reiterate that I know a beautiful and talented person who dated someone for a decade (10 years) before ending the relationship. Although I cannot say it is necessarily a sin to simply date this long, I would ask why is love (and a commitment to marry) taking so long to develop between both parties in this relationship? If, after 10 years, the dating relationship is ended, would not at least one party in the relationship feel severely cheated at having spent a decade in developing (investing in) a relationship that basically disintegrated? How would you feel if after 10 years the person simply decides that they want to marry someone else? Although you might feel like you are going through a divorce, you technically have no legal claim on this person if you have been dating in a pure fashion (e.g., not living together in sin – occupying the same residence). I would be very, very wary of a relationship where I would be expected to date for 10 years before my date would feel comfortable making a marriage commitment.

In my own personal history, there was once a godly young lady whom I dated for some period of time and felt a certain level of serious commitment to. However, in one of our heart-to-heart serious discussions, she shared with me that she might not be ready to make a marriage commitment for some years to come. I believe she said it could possibly be as much as 5 to 10 years before she would be ready; she just was not sure about getting married in general.

As time rocked on, I accepted the fact that I must take this godly lady at her word regarding marriage not being something she was ready for at that period in her life. Thus, my proposal to this dear lady was that we no longer date each other exclusively, that we basically convert our relationship to a friendship where we could call each other from time to time and invite each other out to dinner, but where there was no commitment that would inhibit us from going on dates with whomever we wished. Need I say, in the years to follow, I met someone else, married and had children.

Let me provide a word of caution to you. If you have someone whom you have dated for a considerable period of time and that person expresses great interest in you, be careful not to give the impression that you are indifferent toward the idea of ever marrying, especially if this person possesses the basic virtues/qualities which you desire in a spouse: you could be sabotaging the best marriage prospect ever to come your way.

But you say, Armando (or Rachel) "will always be around when I decide to marry, no matter how cooly I treat him" (or her). Despite the fact that this statement seems to reveal a person who is selfish and inconsiderate (not very Christian-like), it is a fool's idea to believe that no one else in the world will ever pursue interest in Armando (or Rachel), especially when you yourself believe that he (or she) is a nice person.

If I could only count the many persons who have taken their dating relationship for granted, treating their date with coolness and indifference, to later find their date has become disinterested. The date eventually may move on to find someone who believes that he (or she) is the greatest thing since sliced bread.

* * * * * * * * * * * * * * * *

DATING STAGES

I advocate that you not rush too quickly, or unadvisedly, into a serious commitment (e.g., marriage engagement) with someone you are dating.

Some might ask: "What about 'love at first sight'?" It is possible that a person could fall into deep ~~lust~~ love the instance that a person sees someone. But, that still is not the same as the depth of relationship that comes through knowing someone over an extended period of time through all sorts of circumstances: knowing him when he's happy, and knowing her when she's mad ("mad" as in angry, not insane); sharing and mourning with him or her when a loss has occurred, and laughing when things are humorous.

Don't be like the parable below:

> Raul rode with you on the Ferris wheel, or sat next to you on the bus to the church picnic, now "He's your man!, he belongs to you! you own him!" And no other woman better not even smile at him, or she may get a "knuckle sandwich" (a punch in the mouth).

At the same time, I also advocate that you not dally year after year abstaining indefinitely from making a commitment. As these two recommendations (being too hasty or waiting too long) may seem to conflict with each other, you may be wondering what the ideal time period is in which one can expect a serious commitment to develop. Unfortunately, I have not determined a foolproof period of time (e.g., seven months) in which every person will miraculously know if he or she is dating the person that will ultimately be his or her spouse. However, as alluded to earlier in this book, I really have to question the value of a relationship in which one (or both) of the parties is still unsure after 10 years of dating as to whether they should commit to marriage.

The thing that I can do to provide some guideline as to when a serious commitment is appropriate, is to come at your question/concern sideways.

I will come at your question/concern sideways by providing an answer to the following question:

"What are the stages one might go through in this whole dating process?"

Well, for purposes of trying to provide some insight, I will discuss potential stages into which the dating process can be divided. The list of stages that I present do not capture the entire universe of possible ways by which dating can proceed, but the stages I present will hopefully provide a useful framework whereby one can apply the Biblical guidelines discussed in this book.

STAGE 1

The first stage might be called the STRANGER STAGE. Obviously, this stage represents the point prior to your being introduced to someone. "Aha!" you may say, "this is not a dating stage, because all people start out as absolute strangers to each other, and strangers don't have any interaction that is relevant to dating!" I would agree that all people are strangers to each other at some point (except possibly in the case of a mother and child). However, do you not know that the impressions two strangers make on each other can often determine whether they will ever go on a date (or have any sort of relationship, for that matter)?

Let me provide an example of what I mean. There was a single gentleman who was always so insistent that the church ladies greet him with a hug. He would often hold ladies by the hand, patting/massaging their hand, and gazing at them as he doted over them. This gentleman basically developed a reputation as a flirt. Even as I observed this individual, I could understand how he developed this reputation, which resulted in women avoiding him. Especially, as it relates to physical interaction with other people (a greeting, a hug, etc.), one must be very careful in general not to impose oneself on another individual, even when we are speaking of the simple greeting of a hug or kiss on the cheek. The safest route to take with people you do not know well is to give a good firm handshake and, if it is not acceptable etiquette in your circles for a man to shake hands with a lady, a wave of the hand and a good "God Bless You!" is often acceptable.

Some people use spirituality for an excuse for improper physical contact when greeting/meeting people. For example, you may see some gentlemen improperly interpreting IICorinthians 13:12 as a license to corner all the young ladies and demand a "holy" kiss. Biblically speaking, it is actually common for a brother to greet another brother with a kiss on the side of the face (see Luke 22:47 where Judas identifies Jesus to his enemies with a kiss). Just in case you don't have your Bible handy, II Corinthians 13:12 says: "Greet one another with an holy kiss." The concept that Apostle Paul was trying to convey was that he wanted his fellow Christians to greet each other in a pleasant and loving manner.

I don't want to make you paranoid, but you definitely do not want to be misinterpreted as a flirt by people who do not know you, and who take your overly physical greeting the wrong way. And, then again, people who really know you well may still not care for your bone-crushing bearhugs that you give after every single church service.

I want to emphasize that it is important to understand the customs and culture of the people you are interacting with. As long as it is not sinful or dangerous to do so, it is best to consider the customs of the people you find yourself surrounded by.

Let's take a somewhat different example; a parable, if you please:

> Let's say we have a church sister who calls herself Minister Ernie Cook. Minister Cook can often be found Sunday morning at church sitting in the pulpit with the preachers, or sometimes even delivering her message from the Pastor's lectern. When attending Sunday services, it is easy to spot Ernie, as she often wears wool slacks, a suit coat, and a necktie (just like that worn by the senior Pastor and all the associate elders).

Let me be perfectly honest with you: there are many single godly men (godly MANLY men) who would not be interested in meeting (or asking on a date) a woman such as Ernie, who appears to have a slipping grasp on her femininity.

To the brother walking around with long pretty braids and beautiful golden earrings, I say this – you may be scaring away the most eligible holy young women, because you appear to be losing your grip on masculinity. A real woman does not want to marry a man who is more feminine and pretty than she is (I am using the term "man" very loosely here to mean a person born with male reproductive organs, not necessarily one who exemplifies God's model of a man).

Many times people can be discouraged from wanting to be introduced to a potential dating interest because they have observed the person from afar and not liked the impression of what they observed.

Let's say that you see someone and he or she seems to be a good potential date. Since you don't know the person, you are wondering how to meet the person.

Sometimes, the solution is very easy – you may have a mutual friend who you might ask to introduce you to the person. This is only advisable if your friend is discreet and will not embarrass you.

Years ago, a dear saint once volunteered to introduce me to several of the beautiful young ladies of the church where she worshipped. After introducing me to the young ladies, my friend then turned to me and said "Now which one do you want?"

I had not expected such a direct question. This question left me speechless. Fortunately, the young ladies did not appear to hear my friend's question. Or, maybe they just ignored it.

If you have no friends in common with the person that you are interested in meeting, you may need to be a little creative. But be careful, you don't want to appear forward. And, you don't want to say or do something that will embarrass the person you are interested in. And, you don't want to embarrass yourself for that matter.

Take for example one young churchman who saw a young lady at the shopping mall whom he felt attracted to and took a tact such as the following:

Displaying a very bold and confident demeanor, the young

man walks up to her, points at her, and in a suave manner says: "SCORPIO" (As if he knows her astrological sign and thus has some supernatural/mystical connection with her personality).

Let me say that, in the first place, anyone claiming to believe in Christ, is not supposed to follow astrology; Christians should follow Christ. In the second place, the young lady realized that she knew the young man and indicated so to him; by the time that the young man realized he had made such a foolish introduction to a lady who attended a sister church in the same city, he was most embarrassed.

Your creativity may depend on the circumstance in which you have seen the person.

Let me give you two examples of a possible scenario and how you might approach your prospective date:

Scenario 1

> You are at some festive event (e.g., a wedding, or picnic). If the person is not standing sitting near where you are, you might casually drift over to where the person is. If appropriate, you might informally ask him/or her a non-threatening question. For example, if he or she is close to the bowl of potato salad, you might ask: "Is that potato salad in the bowl next to you?" It is not dishonest to ask this question even though you already know it is potato salad. Did not Jesus ask his disciples questions when Jesus already knew the answer? (see Matthew 16:13)

So many people have a "Hollywood" idea of how one must meet someone of the opposite sex. These people think that you have to approach strangers with some incredulously suave (smooth) and witty statement that will make the person you are approaching swoon with adoration. Get Real! Oftentimes, those witty statements that one may have spent hours thinking up (or copying from the Internet), appear corny/ridiculous to the one you are trying to meet. However, if you love risking your ego and you love trying to be witty, go ahead and spin your witty prose to your heart's content. But realize: some people feel imposed upon by perfect strangers approaching them with "witty" remarks. Oftentimes, you may end up embarrassing yourself.

I must strongly advise you to always leave the other person a "way out" if he or she is not interested in carrying on a conversation with you. For example, if you see the other person trying to end the conversation with you, or he or she appears to be totally bored, then you might want to gracefully end the conversation. If the other person says things like, "Well, it has been nice talking with you; I'll be seeing you" 45 seconds after you just began talking, then this might be a clue that the person is not interested in talking with you. Don't get angry or indignant, simply because the person is not interested in continuing a conversation with you. Allow the person to end the conversation. Be courteous. You can say something like: "You take care now; let me go over there and get a soft drink." Do go and get the soft drink whether or not you are thirsty.

Or, if the person is trying to end the conversation but lacks the skill to end it (e.g., he or she doesn't look you in the eyes and repeatedly yawns in an extremely bored fashion), you may want to give the person a "way out" of talking with you. In our picnic example above, you might tell the other person, "Hey let me let you get back to that delicious plate of food. You take care now." If the person is really interested in talking with you, this allows him or her to either indicate that he or she would rather continue talking or that he or she would like to accept your attempt to end the conversation.

As hard as it is for some of you to believe, there are at least a few single people in the universe who actually are not attracted to you as a prospective date. But, don't be totally distraught; just work on being the most godly person you can be and know that God can bless you, even in your desire to date.

In the event that someone is attracted to you and you have absolutely no attraction whatsoever to the person, and he or she is trying to gain your interest in them, don't humiliate and embarrass the person just for the sake of embarrassing him or her, just because you are not interested in them. Remember, if that person is a Christian, he or she is your family member in the Body of Christ. Even if he or she is not a Christian, that person should be treated with common courtesy. Be courteous, but be careful not to be so glowing that the person mistakes your courtesy for mutual interest.

And, let me make an important side point concerning people who will only date individuals that their friends approve as being tall enough, or short enough, or thin enough or heavy enough. These types of physical characteristics, of themselves, do not indicate any lack of godly virtue. Thus, it shows a lack of self-confidence, and over-reliance on friends, when you exclude someone whom you find attractive as a potential date, simply because your friends think he or she has too dark a complexion, your friends think he or she has too light a complexion, your friends think that he is too short, or your friends think that she is too tall. If your friends are so shallow as to judge those you choose to date solely on their God-given physical characteristics, maybe it is time that you had a serious talk with these "friends" regarding their level of maturity.

Again, I am speaking of the physical features that are the result of the genes passed to you from your parents (e.g., the size of your feet). Need I say that a tattoo of the Moon-god on one's forehead is not the type of physical characteristic that I am advocating as having no moral significance. I think it would be good to ask your friend about such an image on his or her date's forehead. Your friend might be dating an idol worshipper.

Scenario 2

You have seen a person you are attracted to ministering (preaching, teaching, singing, worship service musician, etc.). When you see the person in a setting where it is appropriate to have a conversation (e.g., in the lobby after church service), you might approach the person. You might introduce yourself and compliment him or her on the service that he or she rendered (that is, if you truly did enjoy the ministry/service rendered by the person). You might say something like: "Hello, I am Brother Jones. I want to let you know that you really blessed me with that song you sang in the morning session of this convention. Have you recorded any albums?"

Complimenting someone on something that you feel the person did well is often a good way to make an introduction.

STAGE 2

So you have been introduced to (or somehow met) your prospective date. You may have even had a brief conversation with the person. You are now in what I will define as the second stage. I will call this the ACQUAINTANCE STAGE.

When I say that someone is an "acquaintance," I am usually referring to a person whom I have come to know, or someone whom I have been introduced to. When I use the word "acquaintance," I am not referring to a person with whom I have developed a close relationship. When I use the word "acquaintance," I am not referring to a person with whom I am very familiar or have intimate knowledge of.

You may possibly disagree with me. Maybe you just met that "girl of your dreams" today in your college cafeteria. You had lunch with her, talking with each other for hours until the cafeteria had to ask you both to leave so they could close up for the day. From the precious sweet hours of conversation you had together today, you now feel that you know her as well as you know your own blood sister.

Let me make some practical observations:

> 1) As I have mentioned earlier, it takes time to really develop a depth of a relationship. You can love a person, but it takes time to really know him or her in the various facets of his or her personality.

> 2) You never tell someone you just met all of your innermost secrets and personal information. You might as well tape a big sign on your back that says "I am extremely gullible, please come and hurt me!"

But, you say in your mind (or maybe even unconsciously), she is too pretty to have anything but a pure heart. Oh, dear innocent one, what you are doing is relying on a false and dangerous principle that people whom you find physically unattractive are more likely to be evil, and people you find physically attractive are more likely to be holy. You must reject such a false principle. If you don't, you will end up getting into grave trouble, my friend. Do I need to recount the story of the strongest man in the land (Samson of the book of Judges)? If you start reading the 14th chapter of the book of Judges, you will see his weakness for chasing after ungodly women. These women were no doubt beautiful to him; he probably felt these good-looking women could do him no harm, given his supernatural strength. Yet one of these beautiful, ungodly women (by the name of

Delilah) caused his ruin and enslavement to the enemy.

Even if a person is truly holy, how do you know he or she won't accidentally reveal a personal secret that you have prematurely shared? Ideally, your trust for a person should be built up gradually over time; you might try the person with information that is less private at first (information that is generally known about you, and which is not embarrassing to you). Maybe try the person out with some information that is not publicly known, but which won't hurt you severely if your date accidentally spreads your business around town. You will at least have a clue not to reveal anything else to this person that is personal in nature.

As a matter of fact, if a person tells me all of his or her personal business when I first meet him or her, then I have a tendency to label that person in my mind as a Blabber Mouth. You can rest assured that a person who is not discriminating in telling all of his or her personal business upon first meeting you, will definitely share anything that you tell him or her with other people in your community.

While I am on the subject of people with loose lips, let me caution you to be somewhat closed-mouth about sharing details of your dating relationship with persons in your inner circle, unless the persons have a reputation for being discreet. Make sure those you confide in are not Blabber Mouths. Sometimes, close blood relatives can have loose lips. And, if you tell that relative about a crush you have on someone you just met, that relative may have no better intelligence than to go around telling everyone – even the person you have the crush on.

NOTE: a person can be a Christian, even a leader in the church, and have tendencies toward being a Blabber Mouth.

You have made the acquaintance of someone you are interested in. Now you think you are ready to jump right into asking the person to go out with you for an evening of elegant dining. But wait! I suggest you find out more than just a person's first name and marital status (I am assuming the status is "unmarried") before going on a date.

Too often bad dating experiences can be avoided by simply having enough conversation with a person to find out basic facts about the person. No, I am not advocating asking the person a list of detailed personal questions like: "What's your annual income?" That question is appropriate if you are interviewing the person for a job. It is not appropriate to ask of someone you have not known very long. But, if you are simply dating, it might be more appropriate to casually ask the person what line of work he or she is in. If he tells you that he is a "Gangsta Rap artist" you don't even need to know how much money he makes; simply file his name and telephone number in the folder marked "Not a good dating prospect".

Talk about where you both are from, talk about where you both attend church, talk about your hobbies, etc. There are so many subjects one can talk about that don't necessitate that you reveal deep dark secrets, yet give the other person a chance to begin to understand who you are as a person.

Here are some sample questions that you can use to keep the conversation going when you talk with your date:

1) What did you think about the Sunday School lesson last Sunday?

2) Glance at the newspaper and ask your date his or her thoughts on a major current event.

3) What are your three favorite dishes you like to cook?

All these questions, and others like them, will allow you to learn something about your date.

The first one might reveal whether your date attends Sunday School. If asked on several occasions, you may find your date is never attending Sunday School (or any Bible study group); you may need to start wondering about your date's commitment to growing in Christ.

The second question may reveal how much your date is interested in the world around him or her.

The third question might lead into a discussion as to whether your date has domestic/house keeping skills. You may be starry-eyed now and think that he or she is the most perfect being ever, but for people who eventually get married, house keeping skills may be more of an issue than you would think.

There are some things at this stage that you want to make sure you work into your conversation. There are certain things that are public information that would be of keen interest to the other party. I don't think it would be righteous to go out with someone on dates month after month, and when the person becomes emotionally committed to you, you reveal that you have five minor children (children you have been hiding out at grandma's house). The fact that you have five minor children that you are raising is not something from long ago in your past that you simply forgot to mention. You don't have to tell every person you have five children the first instance you meet them. But, if you are asked out on a date, you might casually mention something like: "Well, I would love to go, but I will need to find a babysitter for my children before I say that I can definitely go." This will no doubt elicit questions from the other party as to how many children you have, unless the other party already knows that you have children.

There are other things that may not be public information, yet they are not secrets and would be of keen interest to someone showing an interest in you. For example:

You have accepted a job with a far-away embassy, or you are in the military and you will be shipping out to training or duty far away in several months.

You may have met your acquaintance and had a nice conversation, but you are unsure how to make sure that you will get a chance to talk again. Maybe he is a college student, or businessman visiting from another town. He seems engaged enough in your conversation, but it is time for you to go and he has not asked to call you. Well, my sister, there are ways to keep in contact with this gentleman you just met <u>without</u> being so forward as to say "Can I have your telephone number?" That might (and I say *might*) be okay for a man to do, but I would recommend a more shrewd approach for you sisters.

Ladies (and men too), you could try something like this:

> "Fred, I have really enjoyed meeting you, I am going to have to catch my ride in a couple of minutes. Our church is having a concert next month, if you are interested in attending I could get information on the day and time and let you know the particulars."

If Fred (or whatever his name is) is the least bit interested in you, he will say "Yes, I would like to attend, and he will then give you a telephone number, mailing address, or email address by which to contact him. Now, Fred may say "Yes, I would like to attend." and he may just stand there smiling, mesmerized by your great beauty and charm, not realizing that he has not given you a way to contact him. Well, help him out by saying, "How should I get the information to you?" Now you are set, because this gives you a reason (without seeming forward) to call this gentleman to give him the information regarding the concert; and, if when you contact him, a lengthy conversation develops, so much the better.

Now, if you would allow me to recount how I met my wife, I was introduced to my wife-to-be while visiting some Christian friends far from my home. The next night after meeting my wife-to-be was the New Year's Eve program at the church of my wife-to-be. After the service was over, my wife-to-be and I greeted each other, then I asked her: "What do you and your friends usually do after the New Year's Eve program?" This question gave my wife the opportunity to further our acquaintance without seeming too pushy. Well, fortunately, my wife-to-be said that she and her friends were getting together at one of the local eating establishments that the church people often frequent after church; so, she provided me with directions to meet them there, and we all had a great time talking and eating. As we were all leaving the restaurant to go to our respective cars, I believe I said something like "I'd like to keep in touch". We exchanged telephone numbers, and the rest is history (you know – friendship turning into a relationship, a wedding, a house, kids, etc.)

If my wife-to-be did not wish to continue our acquaintance, she could have diplomatically said something like "Sister Johnson is having a party but I don't think I'll be going." And there was, truthfully, a saint having a get together at her home after the service.

Again, you are seeing my preference not to pressure people into spending time with you. You want to always give the person a chance to gracefully decline. How is it that people think Biblical principles don't apply when dealing with someone we want to date? I want to refer you to the third chapter of the book of James. This chapter is famous for its teaching about the destructive capacity of the tongue (i.e., what we say with our mouths).

Allow me to focus a little further on James, chapter three. Specifically, let's look at verses 13-18:

> 13 Who is a wise man and endued with knowledge among you? let him show out of a good conversation his works with meekness of wisdom.

14 But if ye have bitter envying and strife in your hearts, glory not, and lie not against the truth.

15 This wisdom descendeth not from above, but is earthly, sensual, devilish.

16 For where envying and strife is, there is confusion and every evil work.

17 But the wisdom that is from above is first pure, then peaceable, gentle, and easy to be entreated, full of mercy and good fruits, without partiality, and without hypocrisy.

18 And the fruit of righteousness is sown in peace of them that make peace.

Let me give you the paraphrase of verse 17 that is provided from The Living Bible (TLB):

17 But the wisdom that comes from heaven is first of all pure and full of quiet gentleness. Then it is peace-loving and courteous. It allows discussion and is willing to yield to others; it is full of mercy and good deeds. It is wholehearted and straightforward and sincere.

Pressuring, or embarrassing someone into calling you or going on a date with you is not being "peace-loving and courteous".

I will make up a little parable to dramatize the point I am trying to make:

We have two fictitious characters, Bill and Jane. They are mild acquaintances who attend the same church. One day they happen to sit next to each other during a gospel concert at a public civic auditorium. Bill is attracted to Jane, and strikes up a conversation with her. Jane is polite, but appears distracted from the conversation Bill is trying to hold with her. Bill decides he will discontinue talking so much during the concert and simply try to talk with Jane during the concert's intermission.

During the intermission, Bill sees Jane in the lobby in a long line at one of the tables selling worship music CDs. Bill walks over and tries striking up another conversation. After several minutes of polite conversation, Bill gets up enough nerve to ask Jane to go out on a date next Saturday night.

Jane softly, almost whispering, says: "I appreciate you asking, Bill, but no thank you."

Bill then says: "What about the Saturday after that?"

Jane says: "Thank you, but I would not care to go out."

Bill, in a much louder tone than Jane's tone and volume says: "You mean you don't care to go out with me!"

Jane is becoming embarrassed because people are starting to cast sideways glances at Bill and Jane. Bill sees that Jane is embarrassed, but he does not care.

Bill then says rather loudly: "Can I at least have your phone number, to call you some time?"

Jane, beginning to back away, mutters "I would rather you didn't."

Bill says: "Jane, we go to the same church! You don't have to be so stuck-up!"

Just then an announcement is heard over the intercom that

everyone should return to their seats for the rest of the concert. Bill then turns on his heels in a huff and returns to his seat. Bill, is surprised, and wonders why Jane never returns to her seat next to him.

One week after Bill's performance at the concert in the lobby, he soon finds that his theatrics are known by all of the eligible young ladies at his church. Bill now has the reputation of being a "masher" (a man who attempts to force his attentions on a woman).

As Christians, our bad reputation can be the result of our behaving in a manner that is contrary to the passage of James 3:17, listed earlier.

Don't be fooled; there are some female mashers as well. I have met some in my lifetime. I can recall back even to my teenage years where an acquaintance of mine got this idea in her head that she was going to force me to walk her to her class. This acquaintance literally got my arm in a wrestling lock and refused to let go until I had walked her to class.

So, you have met that godly man, or that godly woman. You both have kept in contact with each other. You have even been going out different places together. You see that he or she seems to have all the basic good qualities that you admire such as a true devotion to God.

STAGE 3

Some time has passed, and you feel that you have developed a relationship with your date that is much more than mere acquaintance.

It may be time for the relationship to move forward a bit.

When I was younger, we used to have a term called "GOING STEADY". This term was used when two people would make a commitment to go on dates together and to spend time together on a regular basis. These two individuals would make a formal commitment to date only each other. This is by no means a marriage commitment; yet it is more than just two acquaintances or friends attracted to each other, deciding to attend social events together.

Even if you are Going Steady, you are not married and the guidelines of proper dating listed in this book still apply (e.g., no rendezvous alone in your date's apartment).

Yes, you have committed to spending time together when you are "Going Steady", yet you must be careful not to become so "clingy" that you smother and suffocate your date, emotionally speaking. If your date can hardly get his or her work done because you constantly call him or her during the day at work, then you are smothering him or her. If you get upset if he or she does not spend every waking moment of his spare time with you, then you are smothering him or her; whether or not he or she realizes it, you are smothering him or her. It may be fun for a while to be smothered by someone, but it will eventually cause you to have a dysfunctional relationship, and a dysfunctional life if the behavior is allowed to continue for too long. Even married couples have to allow each other a certain amount of space and time for themselves, if for no other reason than to allow each of them to have some alone time with God.

Let me also caution you from behaving like married people by making major joint purchases. I have heard of Boyfriend and Girlfriend buying a car together, or a house together. I don't recommend this because you are not committed legally as in a marriage to each other, yet you are binding your financial assets together. So, when you break up (and most of you will experience a break-up one or more times in your life), you have this messy situation of trying to resolve disbursement of the things that you have purchased jointly.

Now, I know that these stages that I describe may seem to be strange to some of my friends who live in cultures where a person's marriage partner is chosen by the family. However, even if your family selects your potential mate, it is your responsibility to get to know that person and ensure that he or she is a godly person with a personality you can be happy living with for the rest of your natural life; when your parents are resting in their graves, and their souls have gone to be with Jesus, you will still be held accountable to stick with that husband or wife until "death do you part".

The dating at this stage is similar to the previous in that you may attend the same types of dating events as before, you may talk on the phone, you may write letters, and etc. However, your friendship with this person becomes more important. There is a stronger emotional tie.

For example, it may be more common and acceptable for both of you to regularly attend each other's family functions/events (i.e., your sister's graduation dinner). Of course, you should be careful not to force people to invite your date to closed family functions. If dad wants to celebrate his birthday with dinner with his children and their spouses, don't force your dad to invite your date if he does not want to. Remember, you may be "Going Steady," but you are not married yet.

Given the commitment and the emotional tie between people "Going Steady," there is more that is required of someone that you are "Going Steady" with, than an acquaintance. Let me make up a parable as an example:

> Your birthday is coming up next month and the person you
> are Going Steady with (let's call him or her your "Steady")

knows that your birthday is on a particular day (Say, the 18th of June). You call your Steady to let him or her know that you will be having a dinner party on your birthday. But your Steady says: "Oh no! the State Fair opens on that day and my school chum and I were thinking about going to see the opening day fireworks. You know how I love fireworks shows." If your Steady is sane and doesn't want more fireworks than he or she bargained for, I would think that he or she would attend your party and pass on the State Fair.

If your Steady knows that it is your birthday (or your graduation, or any other significant event in your life), I would expect him or her, as much as possible, to block out his or her calendar and ask you how he or she can help you celebrate your special day.

Now, a person whom you have gone on dates with occasionally may ask what they can do to help you celebrate your birthday, but he or she is not under the same obligation as your Steady.

There are all sorts of examples I could give, but let me sum it up by saying "Going Steady" is like having a good friend, with whom you are developing an even closer relationship; a good friend who is of the opposite gender, whom you are attracted to in a romantic manner.

STAGE 4

So, you feel that you have dated long enough. You feel like you know your Steady Date very well. You feel that you understand the answer to any number of questions about your special person – questions such as:

What are his or her deepest-held theological/doctrinal beliefs?

What does he or she feel the role of a man versus a woman
is in the home, family and church?
What are his or her goals in life?
What makes him or her happy?
What makes him or her angry/upset?
How does he or she behave when he or she is really upset
with you?
How does he or she handle his or her money?
And so on, and so on…

You feel like you have had a relationship long enough to know the
truth of the answer to these questions and others like them, from
what he or she says and from what he or she does in deed/action.

You feel like you are "In Love" and that you are willing to spend the
rest of your life with this person.

Maybe the subject of marriage has come up in your conversation,
and you both desire to marry each other.

Or, maybe, the man took the lady out and asked her to marry him
over dinner.

And, maybe, you had a dream last night that this beloved person you
are dating is the one that God means for you to marry.

This could be the one for you to marry. However, let me caution you
about dreams and visions. Sometimes, people want to do something
so badly that their mind plays tricks on them and they see visions
and dreams about things they want to do (like getting married).
Sometimes your friends and relatives can have dreams as well that
are based solely on their desire for you to hurry up and get married.

I had a relative who became a widower. There were two different
church ladies greatly interested in him. My relative said that each

of these women were claiming that God had said he was to be their husband. My relative said this: "One of their gods is a lie because God does not mean for me to be a bigamist."

But, let us say that you are sure that this special person you are In Love with is the one you should marry, and you have already taken the time to develop a deep and meaningful relationship. The next step (STAGE FOUR), I will call ENGAGEMENT.

Engagement is when you have come to a point in your relationship that you feel that you should marry each other, and you both commit to marrying each other at some point in the future.

Since you are not married yet, I still charge you to follow the guidelines that I provide in this book (such as the prohibition on intimate physical contact).

Now, when you get engaged you don't have to set a date for your marriage ceremony right away. If you have a date in mind when you get engaged, that is fine as well. But, I do want to advise you to at least set a date far enough in the future for you to utilize the engagement as the final assessment of whether you two should really be together for the rest of your lives.

It is in this final stage that you both will have to do some serious planning and adjusting in preparation for your life together after marriage. It is under the stress of engagement that many relationships fall apart.

There are yet some little surprises that may come out during the engagement that you were not aware of. Things such as he promised his mother that she could live with him, even after he married a bride. You may not have been aware of this until you started planning your life together. Actually, he may not even remember he said it, because it was a promise he made so many years ago. Yet, mama remembers, and you both will need to find a way to work through this issue. Maybe this is not a big deal for you, but it would be a major issue for many.

Or, you are in the normal child-rearing years, but you know that you are physically incapable of fathering children. Will your wife be able to handle this fact? Well, you'd better share this information with her, and find out if she can handle it before you get married. For many women (and men), not being able to have natural children is a show-stopper, as far as getting married is concerned.

For those of you getting engaged, I would suggest (no matter how good your relationship is) that you schedule a few counseling sessions with an experienced Christian marriage counselor before you even set a wedding date. Too often, an objective marriage counselor can identify some major issues that an engaged person would simply overlook or brush past, only to later regret.

An experienced marriage counselor can do such things as walk you each through a thorough, objective Compatibility Assessment. An experienced counselor can then identify the strengths and weaknesses of your relationship. Your counselor can even give you some intensive coaching on how to deal with the shortcomings in your relationship and in your personality. Your counselor can help you develop techniques that will help you throughout your married life – techniques such as better communication skills (e.g., listening and saying what you mean in a less antagonistic manner).

An experienced marriage counselor may even help you learn some things about yourself that you did not realize – revelations such as attitudes you have as a result of baggage you are carrying from a previous relationship. Maybe your husband ran off to Tahiti and left you with 3 young children to raise alone; this may have caused some deep scars in your life that are affecting your ability to trust the godly man you are now engaged to marry. Your counselor may be able to help you "scan" your baggage (i.e., issues) you brought from a previous relationship(s) and assist you in throwing out those weights that will destroy your marriage.

You may have thought that you had the subject of children nailed down tight. He wants three and you want three, and you both will accept boys or girls, or a mix of the two. However, counseling sessions will help you discover some points you may have missed. For example: you are both in your mid-30s now, and he wants to wait 10 years before you both start trying to have your first of three children, because he is trying to get his business off the ground right now and doesn't have time for kids yet. For many women, this would be a major issue, trying to have three kids while between the ages of 45 and 50.

In my imagination, I can hear some of you brothers saying right now that: "I know all there is to know about my fiancée." Dear brother, this type of statement is most naïve. There are people who have a good marriage and have been married 25 years or more, who could not say that they know all there is to know about their spouse. Yet, after a few years, or even a few months, you feel you have exhausted all there is to know about your future spouse? Don't let your ego or stubbornness prevent you from getting counseling.

Dear one, even if you know everything, wouldn't you want your fiancée to have a chance to make sure she understands you as well as possible? Get counseling, even if you have to pay for it. Dear Brother, what are you trying to hide, anyway? Before my wife married me, I wanted her to understand everything she could about my personality, my vision, my style of leadership in the home – I did not want to trick her into marrying me. I wanted her to have a realistic view of the relationship that she would have with me, even if it meant the risk of losing her. Deception, or even a mistaken view concerning the essence of a person, is not the foundation of a good marriage.

In my imagination, I can hear some of you sisters say: "If it is going to cost money, I don't think I can afford it." Dear Sister, let me ask you three questions: "How much will your wedding dress cost?", "How much will your ring cost?" and "How much will your wedding ceremony and reception cost?" I could go on with this line of questioning, but the point that I am trying to make is that the central, most important thing that you should be investing time and money in is making sure that you are building a healthy relationship that will last a lifetime, because a divorce is very expensive – emotionally, spiritually and financially.

I would rather you rent a wedding dress, buy a ring made of tin, make your own cake and have it served with ice water, and take the time and spend the money to get adequate counseling before jumping into a life-long commitment of marriage. Too often, people planning to get married think that a wedding is supposed to be a big, ostentatious show of materialistic wealth and conspicuous consumption – as if "the bigger the show, the more successful the marriage will be."

Aw, my friend, all you have to do is look to the Southern part of the region I live in, and see that money and a big wedding did not prevent so many Hollywood stars from failing to have an enduring and peaceful marriage. It is so much more important to ensure that a person is marrying the right individual. And, even if you have found the right individual, it is so important that you build a solid relationship – which often means getting pre-marital counseling. And, that may mean more than just one counseling session – you may need a whole series of sessions. Better to get all the significant "issues" and problems aired out now, than after the honeymoon (when all of the honey seems to have dripped out of the moon and you come to the reality that your beloved is a lot less perfect than you thought while dating him or her).

Don't misunderstand my comments about spending money on

a wedding. I do believe that Christians should try to have a nice wedding. A wedding is a beautiful and noble culmination of your dating relationship with your beloved and represents your holy commitment to spend the rest of your life together. Your wedding should reflect this fact. I strongly encourage individuals not to elope. When two Christians run off and marry secretly, they usually later regret not having had a wedding. So, I encourage you to have a wedding, have an extravagant and beautiful one – but do it within the financial limitations that you can afford. If you ever want to know what eternity feels like, start your marriage with a mountain of debts.

Let me return to this question of counseling. With some of you, it may be important to get more than pre-marital counseling. If you have been abused, assaulted or suffered other deep traumatic experiences in your past, I recommend that you also see a Christian psychologist to ensure that you have really recovered from the experience. I recommend this, even if you feel you have recovered and feel that you don't need any help. You owe it to yourself (and to your spouse-to-be) to be as mentally and emotionally fit as you can be as you move into the lifetime commitment of marriage.

Speaking of being fit, I would also recommend that you get a full physical checkup as well. If you have health problems, I think it is only fair to disclose this to your future spouse before you two get married.

People sometimes make the mistake of thinking people have to be mentally insane before they can benefit from counseling. Going to see a Christian psychologist or counselor does not mean that you are on the verge of committing mass-murder. If your associates hold to such backward views regarding getting Christian psychological counseling, I still advise you to go; but, you can simply not tell your acquaintances that you are getting counseling. Everyone does not need to know your personal business.

Consider the following verse, which talks about counselors:

"Without counsel purposes are disappointed: but in the multitude of counsellors they are established." (Proverbs 15:22)

Let me put this verse in modern terms. Plans can fail or flop because of lack of counsel. I have used many counselors throughout my life: Pre-marriage counselor, financial counselor, school counselor, career counselor, infant care counselor, real estate counselor, etc.

But, make sure to choose your counselors well, for advice from an unwise counselor can make a mess of your life.

An engagement should be a time of great joy and excitement, if you are certain you have found the one that God means for you to commit your life to. Despite your great excitement over the prospect of marrying your beloved, you need to eventually get down to some serious planning.

For one thing, you will at some point need to plan your wedding. Now as far as planning a wedding, my personal opinion is that both the bride and groom should play the key decision-making roles in the planning. Of course, the family and friends can provide advice and even hands-on help, but I believe sometimes family members can hijack a wedding to the extent that the bride and groom are only incidental participants. Regardless of who is paying for the wedding, I think it is important for the wedding to give an engaged couple the feeling that the wedding is something that they are working on together. And, planning a wedding often provides those stressful and awkward situations that allow you additional opportunities to see how your beloved functions under pressure.

The following parable might illustrate what I mean by stressful and awkward situations:

Ben and Sarah are engaged to be married. Ben's favorite Uncle, Uncle Bud, asks Sarah and Ben if he could play an instrumental rendition of The Lord's Prayer as part of the wedding services.

Sarah then asks: "What instrument do you play?"

Uncle Bud tells her that he plays the banjo.

Ben likes the banjo, but is not thrilled with the idea of a banjo rendition of The Lord's Prayer being performed as part of his wedding ceremony.

Sarah, on the other hand, totally hates the idea.

How Ben and Sarah resolve this and other wedding planning issues allow excellent opportunities for the couple to reaffirm, or raise doubt, as to whether each are compatible with the other.

Yet, there are other planning issues that must be worked out before marriage, which are even more important than the wedding ceremony – such as:

Where will you live?
Oh! You just assumed that you both would live with his parents? Have you both talked this out with his parents before making that assumption? What are the house rules, conditions, expectations of living at his parents' house? Have you talked these out with his parents? When you begin to investigate your assumptions, you may find them to be invalid: his parents may have expected that you would be getting your own apartment; they may actually have been looking forward to having the entire house to themselves.

What transportation will you both use?
Can you both really afford to buy a car, or two cars (one for each of you)? You might both have to come to some sort of agreement concerning both of you using public transportation until you are able to afford a car.

What sort of household budget will you both live by?
If neither of you know how to plan a household budget, you better find someone fast who is experienced at doing budgets – someone who will help you develop one now, and who will also be there to help you after you get married. Among the rich, poor and middle classes, how each person in a marriage spends money is often a contributing factor as to why a marriage fails. Going through the budget-planning exercise now can really help you know whether your fiancé/ fiancée is the "Right Man" or the "Right Woman".

Next, I need to bring up a really touchy situation with regards to planning. Some of you who are dating possess significant material resources (e.g., a house, property, cash, a family business or other resources). And, to complicate things a bit more, some of you may have heirs (children) who are not the offspring of the person you are engaged to marry. I would strongly recommend that if you have any assets, that you sit down with your own personal Christian professional financial/legal advisor, and discuss all of the tough questions, such as how to ensure your wishes are carried out regarding what your children will receive in the event of your death. I definitely recommend setting up your trust, will or whatever other legal documents are necessary, according to the advice of your professional financial/legal counselor.
Then, I would recommend that you sit down with your fiancé/fiancée and your advisor and step through how your estate is organized.

If your fiancé/fiancée insists or event hints that he or she expects to receive all that you have accumulated prior to meeting him or her, upon your death, I would think twice about the marriage. He or she may be what we call a "Gold Digger" – someone who searches for a victim to marry, who has material wealth, in hopes of getting his or her hands on the victim's gold (wealth). Don't be fooled; a Gold Digger can trick the victim into thinking he or she has met his or her true love. But, the Gold Digger cares little for the victim, and is just after the gold and luxuries that wealth can buy.

If you find that you cannot resolve important money matters prior to marriage, don't expect money issues will disappear or resolve themselves after you get married.

There are so many issues that should be discussed when seriously considering marrying a person, that these issues are too numerous to list. However, one issue that should be discussed thoroughly is the rearing of minor step-children.

> Will the children live with you and your spouse after you are married?

> Will the children spend time with the other natural parent, grandparents, relatives?

> What about discipline? Do you and your spouse believe in corporal punishment?

> How do each of you define proper corporal punishment? Under what circumstances will each of you administer punishment?

The questions above are just a few things that you should discuss. Although kids should not be the sole factor in determining who you marry, kids should definitely not be ignored when becoming involved in a relationship with someone. Life can become a living nightmare when marrying someone who does not get along with your children;

especially if you have a teenager. (If you agree heartily with what I just said, say "Amen!" real loud right where you are.)

After you get into some of the serious pre-marriage planning that engaged people should do, you may come to the conclusion that he or she is not the one you should be marrying. Don't go through with marrying the person, just because you have set a date and sent out the invitations. Also, don't go through with the wedding because you allowed yourself to fornicate and get pregnant.

It is foolish to marry the wrong person and just hope that God's gonna work a miracle after I marry this scoundrel and turn the proverbial frog into a prince or princess. Marrying that person probably won't change him or her at all.

Getting married is not a joke or a game, or something you can simply and easily quit if you find you don't like it. I want you to meditate on the types of vows made during wedding ceremonies. Below, I have provided a version similar to those used frequently in Christian weddings. If you are the man, think about the holy promises that are required of the man in the vows below. If you are the woman, think about the holy promises that are required of the woman below. Then look at the vows that your beloved must make – do you feel that you both are willing and capable of fulfilling these vows – for the rest of your whole entire lives (whether that be 10, 50, or 100 years)?

> MARRIAGE VOWS:
> THE MINISTER SAYS TO THE MAN:
> "(*The Man's Name*), will thou have this woman to be thy wedded wife? To live together after God's providence in the holy state of matrimony? Will thou love her, comfort her, honor and keep her in sickness and in health; and, forsaking all others for her alone, perform unto her all the respect that a husband owes to his wife, so long as you both shall live?"

THE MAN IS SUPPOSED TO SAY: "I will."

THE MINISTER SAYS TO THE WOMAN:
"(*The Woman's Name*), will thou have this man to be thy
wedded husband? To live together after God's providence in
the holy state of matrimony? Will thou obey him, serve him,
love, honor, and keep him, in sickness and in health, richer
or poorer, better or worse and forsaking all others for him,
will perform unto him all the duties that a wife owes to her
husband, as long as you both shall live?"

THE WOMAN IS SUPPOSED TO SAY: "I will."

Many weddings include a Ring Service as part of the wedding that
goes something like this:

THE MINISTER HOLDS UP THE MAN'S AND
WOMAN'S WEDDING RINGS AND SAYS:

"The wedding ring is an external and visible sign signifying to
all the uniting of this man to this woman in Holy matrimony
through the Church of Jesus Christ our Lord."

[The minister then gives the man the ring to place on the
third finger of the woman's left hand. The man holds his
hand on the woman's ring that he placed on her finger and
repeats the following after the minister]:

"In token of our commitment and abiding love, with this ring
I thee wed, in the Name of the Father, and of the Son, and of
the Holy Ghost. Amen."

[The minister then gives the woman the ring to place on
the third finger of the man's left hand. The woman holds

her hand on the man's ring that she placed on his finger and repeats the following after the minister]:

"In token of our commitment and abiding love, with this ring I thee wed, in the Name of the Father, and of the Son, and of the Holy Ghost. Amen."

THE MINISTER HAS THE MAN AND WOMAN JOIN HANDS AND PLACES HIS HAND ABOVE THEIRS AND SAYS:

"Forasmuch as (The Man's Name) and (The Woman's Name) have bound themselves together in Holy Wedlock, and have solemnized their matrimonial vows before God and this audience, and thereto have declared the same by joining hands and by giving and receiving rings: I proclaim that they are husband and wife together, in the name of the Father, and of the Son, and of the Holy Ghost. Those whom God has joined together, let no man separate.

Amen."

Think about these vows often during your engagement. Meditate on whether both of you really have the ability and determination to keep them.

If you are the least bit fuzzy about, or if you have any question whatsoever about any word listed in these vows, please ask your Christian marriage counselor to explain these vows to you before you decide to set a wedding date. God and the community, and most of all, your spouse, should be able to count on you to keep these vows until you die if you make them.

STAGE 5

I want to talk about one more stage that one might not consider a relationship or dating stage at all. Yet, I must share at least a few choice words regarding BREAKING UP.

A discussion of Breaking Up is most relevant to two individuals who are either Going Steady or who are Engaged. I mention these two stages because these are the stages which I have defined as each party having a commitment to be together. With an acquaintance, or even a friend with whom you are not Going Steady, you may go out with him or her from time to time. However, if you don't go out with the person for months, you have not necessarily broken off a commitment. I have had friends whom I have gone on a date with and simply drifted apart; we still remain friendly toward one another. But, due to reasons (which may have been purely virtuous), we found other people we desired to go out with.

Again, I don't necessarily classify it as a Break-up if you wish to stop going on dates with an acquaintance. If there is a particular/specific reason why you no longer wish to go on dates with an acquaintance whom you have gone out with in the past, you may need to share that reason with your acquaintance, especially if your acquaintance is still strongly interested in going out with you. For example, it may have been several months since you have seen your acquaintance, and since that time you have started Going Steady with someone. It is just a matter of courtesy not to allow someone you have dated in the past to continue to pursue you when you have a definite reason why you are definitely not interested in going on any further dates. This specific piece of advice that I give here is for instances where the acquaintance has treated you with at least a minimum of decency and respect – for example, if you had to end a date with an acquaintance because he or she was abusive to the point of threatening physical harm, or he or she tried to pressure you into some sinful act, you might be justified in never calling the person again (not even to return his or her calls).

With regards to real Break-ups (between people Going Steady or Engaged to be married), I would urge the utmost care in how you execute the Break-up. Yes, Breaking Up is often a necessity, but how one does it will determine whether or not you have maintained proper consideration for the other person's feelings.

When you are considering breaking off a relationship, one of the things you should do is sit down and prayerfully formulate in your mind exactly why you are breaking off the relationship. The fact that he bought you a one-carat diamond engagement ring and you wanted a two-carat ring may not be a sufficient reason to break off the relationship. Ask God to help you determine if it is appropriate to break off your relationship. List in your mind all the reasons why you believe you should break up. Maybe you should even get some counsel from your spiritual mentor concerning your intent to break off the relationship.

I caution you not to use the threat of breaking off the relationship as a way to control your friend. If you are constantly threatening to break off your relationship to get your friend to behave appropriately towards you, you should consider not dating that person anymore. It sounds to me as though this just isn't the right person for you, if they will only do what is right when there is an impending threat that you will break off the relationship.

Don't break up with someone for frivolous reasons. For example: you borrowed your boyfriend's car to go shopping with some friends. You got back so late that you made your boyfriend late for work. He is angry with you and says that you cannot borrow his car again unless you promise to be back in time for him to get to work in a timely fashion. Your pride gets the best of you, and you threaten to break up with him. I have simply two words for you, my dear sister: GROW UP! You have a boyfriend who was gracious enough to lend you his car; you are in a relationship with someone responsible enough to want to be on time to work; and, you have someone willing to forgive you and let you use the car again under reasonable conditions. What you really need to do is apologize and humbly (with a sweet attitude) ask your boyfriend to forgive you. If you cannot ask forgiveness when you have wronged someone, you really should break up with your boyfriend, because you are not fit to have a relationship with anyone.

Many relationships break off because of the immature behavior of one, or both parties involved.

Let's say you feel clearly that you should break up with your friend or fiancé/fiancée. You have prayed and discussed the issue with one of the wise Christians in whom you have confidence, and you feel it is time to share with your friend or fiancé/fiancée that you would like to end the relationship.

Breaking up does not mean the same thing to all people. And, it does not mean the same thing in all situations.

Long ago, there was a godly woman whom I dated, and we eventually decided to Go Steady. I had, and still have, a great deal of respect for this attractive, godly woman. However, it became clear after some time that this godly woman did not foresee marriage as something in her immediate future. To put it in her words – she did not know whether she would be ready to get married in 5 years or even 10 years. We did not call each other ugly names, we did not say to each other "I'll never speak to you again!" Our break-up took the form of me suggesting that we not commit ourselves to going out only with each other. My suggestion was that we could still go on dates and call each other, but that we not feel committed to going out only with each other. Oh, the reason for me breaking up? Well, my time horizon for getting married was just too different from my friend's.

There are some situations where you will want to break up with a person and you will never want to go on a date with them again. Let's say that your boyfriend is such a flirt that you cannot go to the restroom during dinner without his trying to get a date with the waitress while you are gone. This guy, you will want to break up with, and not even go on dates with on an occasional basis.

So, you are clear that you want to break off the relationship and you have an idea of what you would like your contact with him or her to be after the break-up (e.g., no contact whatsoever, talk on the phone only, go on dates occasionally, or some other option). If you want to continue some contact, just remember that the other party may choose not to have any contact with you.

Now for the hard part. You must communicate to the other party your desire to break up. I generally don't recommend breaking off a relationship by sending a letter or email. However, if you fear any physical or verbal abuse from the other party, a letter or email may be the best way.

Sometimes breaking up is better done via phone than in person. Some of the quietest people you know may become irate and uncontrollably upset at the prospect of losing a love interest. Consider jotting down on paper, or making mental notes, as to what you want to say. You should communicate that you want to break up and the reason in a manner that is respectful, as much as possible, of the other person's feelings. For example, the guy you may be dating is lazy, doesn't want to work, and expects you to work every day after you are married, while he lives the lifestyle of the rich and famous. Regardless of your temptation to do so, you probably shouldn't tell him that he is a "Lazy, Selfish, Bum". You might start by telling him something like: "I feel that we need to end our relationship. The plain truth is that I am looking for someone much more industrious; someone that enjoys putting in a hard day's work." Try not to get into name-calling and personal attacks.

If you do choose to break up with someone in a face-to-face setting, by all means, choose an appropriate setting. Way off in some deserted place is not an appropriate location. Taking a drive in the woods, or an abandoned parking lot, or at his or her apartment is not an appropriate place for you both to be alone, even if both of you never plan to break up. I would suggest that you both have a way to get home independently of each other – I won't say this is mandatory, but it is just wise. For one thing, you don't want to be dependent on someone to get you home safely who feels like you have just "dumped" him or her. Also, even with Christians, breaking up does leave hurt feelings, and the other person may not want to see you for a while.

When breaking up, try to focus in on exactly what your issue is, in a respectful manner. Otherwise, you may end up not only breaking up, but creating an enemy of someone who would have continued to be your friend after the break-up. The other person may not understand why you want to break up, no matter how much you explain over and over your reasons for breaking off the relationship. Sometimes, this is the result of the other person not wanting to understand, because he or she does not want to break up. However, do not stay in the relationship if you are certain and sure that you should break up, even if the other person does not wish to break up. You may have to exhibit a certain amount of fortitude and firmness to stick to your decision, as some people will try to pressure you into staying in a relationship through such various control tactics as guilt, blackmail, or plays on your sympathy.

One way that a person might use guilt is to list all the things that he or she has done for you during your relationship. He or she may recount all of the exorbitant amounts of money that were spent on you. He or she may claim that you were only using them, that you have betrayed him or her. (As a side note, in any relationship, you should make it a practice not to spend excessive amounts of money on anyone that you are not married to. And, you should not allow someone you are dating to recklessly spend money on you. Moderate tokens are okay, but extravagant spending will most often come back to haunt you (e.g., when you decide to break up).)

One way that a person might use blackmail is to threaten to share some deep secret of yours if you break up with him or her. God forbid that you have been sexually impure with your date; he or she may threaten to expose your fornication if you break off the relationship. Or maybe he or she threatens to spread lies that you were sexually impure, when you really weren't. Whether it be true, or not (that you have been sexually impure), blackmail is not a healthy reason to continue in a relationship. Some people have gone as far as to marry someone that they did not love because a child was conceived outside of wedlock. To this I say, stop fornicating, both of you bear your responsibility for taking care of the child emotionally and financially – but conceiving a child is no indication that you should get married.

One way that a person might try to get you to change your mind regarding breaking up with him or her is to play on your sympathy. This can take many forms. She or he might feign being ill and even commit himself or herself to the hospital (or he or she might indeed really be sick). However, the fact that you feel sorry for the person is not the basis of a healthy relationship, when you know the relationship has other insurmountable issues. He or she might even become so emotionally upset about the break-up that he or she goes on a hunger strike for days on end. (Really, I am not joking!) This ought to confirm something to you about your friend. Do you really need to be romantically involved with someone who borders on being suicidal?

I once broke up with a church lady who had been extremely cruel to me during the latter part of our relationship. This lady had the audacity to use the principle of "forgiveness" as a means to try and get back into a relationship with me. Let me help you understand something: you can forgive a girlfriend or boyfriend who treats you badly, but that does not mean the damage done to your relationship goes away. You can truly love someone as Christ says to love and still not want to reconcile (or revive) a romantic relationship with someone who has conducted himself or herself inappropriately. As for my friend that I mentioned above, I told her that I wished the best for her (I truly did forgive her and cared about her), yet I was not willing to reconcile our romantic relationship; the type of person she was inside, was just not the kind of person God meant for me to be with – she simply was too much of a spiritual drain and distraction from my walk with God.

I told my friend that if she would really get herself together, that I might in the future be willing to introduce her to some eligible young men. But, she and I were not going to be more than simply friends.

Perhaps you don't believe me when I tell you forgiveness does not always mean restoration of a relationship to the trust and intimacy experienced prior to the offence. Let me give you an example of something that can happen to a Christian:

> You have a relative who fell on hard times. You brought him into your home to live until he could get on his feet. While you were at work, he sold everything out of your home that was not nailed down, and then fled before you returned home. Weeks later, the police arrest him in a department store trying to use credit cards stolen from your home.
> Your relative asks you to forgive him and says it would not be right for you to let the police put him in jail if you really forgive him.

> Does forgiveness always mean that wrong-doers should never face the consequences of their actions? Should every criminal standing before a judge be let free if he or she says

"I am sorry for what I did"?

> I am not advocating that you hate your relative. But, I do think your relationship with your relative may change. Even when he gets out of jail, you may no longer trust him to be in your house when you are not present. You love him, but that deep trust is broken and may (or may not) take a long time to ever revive.

Now, there is the possibility that your reason for wanting to break up is based on your perception, as opposed to fact. Let me give you a parable:

> Your "Steady" has been offered a position doing research for Harvard University. But, you both currently live in California. Your Steady is exuberant (filled with excitement) about the position and has already called across country to her new employer and accepted the position. You debate long and hard in your mind, and even pray concerning whether you can handle a long-distance relationship. You finally decide to break the news to your Steady that you feel that it would be more than you could handle to try and maintain your relationship indefinitely, separated by thousands of miles.

> However, much to your surprise, you find that your Steady only has to physically be at Harvard for an initial six weeks of training – most of the research work will take place in California. She apologizes for failing to mention this fact, and all is well.

So, leave some room for the possibility that you have misinterpreted the facts concerning the need to break off the relationship.

Be careful when breaking up. No matter how respectfully you deal with the person you are breaking up with, he or she may feel rejected and hurt, and wish to try and hurt you back. People seeking revenge against someone who has broken off a relationship is, unfortunately, not uncommon among people who attend church. Your girlfriend or boyfriend may feel that if he or she cannot have you, then he or she will ruin your reputation through lies and rumors so that no one else will have you. However you deal with this, do not stoop to un-Christian-like behavior. Maintain your integrity. Don't resort to revenge against the person. Don't retaliate by spreading rumors and lies of your own. And, by all means, don't send your buddies over to his or her house to rough him or her up a bit. (Some church people feel that it is okay to send their sinner-friends to assault someone for them).

What if the other person is initiating a break-up with you? Well, I think the guidance I give in this section is still good advice. Even if the other person is the one initiating the break-up, you still want to be respectful and considerate of the other person. You still want to listen carefully and focus on the reason that your friend desires to break off the relationship. If you feel that your friend's concerns are based solely on perception rather than reality, discuss where you think your friend has misunderstood you, or your actions. But, focus on the issues and do not let your discussion degenerate into a contest to see who can throw the most hurtful insult.

By all means, if the other party insists on breaking up, even if you don't agree that you should break off the relationship, you must respect his or her wishes. As a Christian, you are not allowed to force someone against his or her will to date you – that would be the height of selfishness to do so.

CONCLUSION:

Having spent a considerable amount of time discussing breaking up in Stage 5, let me say that breaking up is not always the natural conclusion of a relationship. Many of you have, or will, find the right person for you. And, through your ups and downs of the dating relationship, you will advance to the point of committing yourselves to each other in holy matrimony (marriage). And, some of you may choose never to marry; that's okay, too.

> I would like for you to meditate on the words of Apostle Paul in the following verses (I Corinthians 7:6-7):
>
> 6 But I speak this by permission, and not of commandment.
>
> 7 For I would that all men were even as I myself. But every man hath his proper gift of God, one after this manner, and another after that.

The Living Bible (TLB) explains these verses thus:

> 6 I'm not saying you must marry; but you certainly may if you wish.
>
> 7 I wish everyone could get along without marrying, just as I do. But we are not all the same. God gives some the gift of a husband or wife, and others he gives the gift of being able to stay happily unmarried.

Whether you are single or married, I encourage you to live your life to the glory of God. If you desire be married, seek God about your desires and consider the guidelines of this book. If you decide to stay single, there are also advantages to being single and not having the obligations of meeting the needs of a spouse. Whatever you do, make sure you are in God's divine will if you want to get the most out of life.

By the way, there are two free bonus features that I have included as attachments at the end of this book. Both of these attachments are based on articles completed well before I began writing this dating guide. Thus, the attachments may seem somewhat distinct from the book itself. However, I include these two attachments as they address various Biblical concepts that relate to male-female relationships.

The attachments are:

ATTACHMENT A
[Christians Dating non-Christians]

ATTACHMENT B
[What the Christian Man is looking for in a Woman]

* * * * * * * * * * * * * * * *

ATTACHMENTS

ATTACHMENT A

[Christians Dating non-Christians]

My friends, I need to talk with you about this idea of Christians dating non-Christians. I first need to tell you that this dangerous practice is nothing new. Grab your Bible and take a look at IICorinthians 6:14. It reads as follows:

> Be ye not unequally yoked together with unbelievers: for what fellowship hath righteousness with unrighteousness? and what communion hath light with darkness?

The Living Bible (TLB) gives a paraphrase of this verse that reads as follows:

> Don't be teamed with those who do not love the Lord, for what do the people of God have in common with the people of sin? How can light live with darkness?

Now, in case you're incorrectly thinking that this verse means that you cannot have neighbors or co-workers who are not Christians, read I Corinthians 5:10.

The point here is that God does not intend for your heart, soul and mind to become so entangled with someone who has not placed Christ at the head of his or her life. Yes, I know there are people that have married, and established a family, then accepted Christ as their Savior afterwards, while their spouse remains a sinner. Paul encourages the Christian to stay devoted to the spouse who is not a Christian, if the non-Christian is willing to stay in this marriage relationship (see I Corinthians 7:12-16).

So, you might think: "what's the difference from me dating and possibly marrying someone who is not a Christian? What's the difference from the person above where one of the persons became a Christian after getting married?"

Okay, let me tell you again: when you date someone, your heart, mind and soul has the potential of being entangled with that person, even before engagement or marriage, which might come later. A person who is not a Christian is a servant of sin and you are a servant of righteousness (Romans 6:16 and 6:18). Can't you see the heartache you are walking headlong into, by dating someone who cannot even understand the most important relationship in your life (i.e., your relationship with Christ)?

If you know someone who truly puts Christ first in their life, yet has a spouse who is not a Christian, see if you can get them to tell you generally how it is, being married to a non-believer. If they feel comfortable sharing with you, they may say like the prophet Jonah: "out of the belly of hell cried I" (Jonah 2:2). Being married to a non-believer can be like living with Satan himself.

And, if you are really a Christian, you want to obey what the Bible says, which tells us only to marry in the Lord (marry only another Christian) (I Corinthians 7:39).

Yes, I know some make all sorts of creative excuses for dating non-Christians. For example, the old fashioned, worn-out excuse that the Christian is proselytizing/converting the non-Christian, and that the Christian is not romantically involved.

This type of dating is also very unwise, because there is a high probability that the non-Christian has some attraction to the Christian; and, when the non-Christian comes to the realization that you really have been dating him or her to convert them and have absolutely no interest in them romantically, you may not only lose your convert, but gain an enemy.

You may gain this person as an enemy, or at least offend them, even if you caution them that you are only dating them to convert/witness about Jesus. By simply dating someone, people will naturally hold on to hope that there is a possibility of a relationship developing.

And then, the Christian may still fall for the non-Christian; By the sheer fact of dating someone, there is the possibility of falling into a relationship, even when that is not the original intent. That is why a Christian who is married does not go out on dates with anyone other than his or her spouse.

Do me a favor and try this: ask a close married Christian friend of yours, maybe your Pastor, if he would consent to other men dating his wife if she promised not to fall in love with the men who wanted to date her. Does this sound like a ridiculous question to even ask? Of course it does. I think you get the point.

Finally, so many Christian ladies say they have to date non-Christians because there are so few men in the church. Let me let you in on a little secret: so many true Christian men become discouraged in looking for Christian ladies to date because many in the physical sanctuary are not necessarily virtuous (see Proverbs 31: 10-31).

Simply put, if you love God, you will do things his way and not your way (John 14:15, Proverbs 14:12).

ATTACHMENT B

This attachment is based on an article that was completed well before I began writing the Holiness.com Dating Survival Guide. I originally wrote the article at the request of one of the dear Christian ladies of my family who urged me to write about what Christian men are looking for in a woman.

For those of you who purchased this book and have enjoyed the style of presentation, feel free to visit Holiness.com and let me know if you would like to see an attachment addressing what Christian ladies are looking for in a man in a future edition of this book.

If I get enough positive responses, I might be encouraged to have one of the gifted Christian ladies in my circle write an article concerning what Christian ladies are looking for in a man. Judging from the men that I have counseled, many of the Christian men in the body of Christ might greatly benefit from such an article.

[What the Christian Man is looking for in a Woman]

Part 1 and Part 2

Part 1

Well, the previous discussion on dating has prompted additional questions. Just A Sister asks: "What is the Christian man looking for in a woman?" Let's consider this question for a little while. I will render an answer to the question, but let us just prayerfully think on this very valid question for now.

[**NOTE**: "Just A Sister" is a pseudonym that reflects the publication of ideas, comments, and questions submitted by various sisters (i.e., Christian ladies).]

Okay, we have considered the question of what a brother is looking for and, what follows is a beginning to the answer.

What you are reading now is the first installment of the answer to the question "What are Christian brothers looking for?" If you would allow me to do so, I would like to rephrase this question as follows: "What are mature Christian brothers looking for?" What is sought after in this question is a guide or general tips as to what mature Christian brothers are looking for in a prospective wife. In our context here, "mature" is not defined by one's chronological age. "Mature," in this context, refers to one who has developed to an advanced state of wisdom and discipline in living true to Biblical principles, even when great sacrifice is necessary to live by these principles. This is not to say that an immature Christian brother does not have a desire to marry. However, the selection criteria of a mature Christian brother is likely to be a much better guide of what the Bible would have a Christian man to seek after in a potential spouse. Before attempting to speak on the question, I must first provide an admonition regarding my answer. The admonition is as follows:

The original question was asked in the context of dating and marriage in certain Christian communities within the larger American society. Therefore, certain customs referenced in this discussion may be unfamiliar to individuals of other cultures. For example, in my culture, the choice of whom one marries is left primarily to the discretion of the man and woman deciding to marry. Although such customs may not be prevalent in all cultures, any Biblical principles outlined in the context of discussing these customs are applicable to all people around the globe. For example, the Biblical principle of being kind to one another (Ephesians 4:32) must be applied within cultures and customs that adhere to dating before marriage, as well as cultures that do not.

I. APPEARANCE. To begin our discussion, the first thing (but not necessarily the most important thing) that generally catches a brother's attention is the appearance or visual attractiveness of a sister. Now, one might say that it is sinful for a single man to find a single lady attractive. To this, I would challenge one to show what sin has taken place because of a simple attraction. Where sin might possibly come into play is when a person does, or says something that promotes/tempts himself or herself to express that attraction in a manner that is only appropriate for married couples to express their love to each other (see Hebrews 13:4).

As "beauty" is a very subjective thing, it is almost impossible to define an exact universal standard of what all Christian brothers view as visually attractive. Having understood this fact, I will give general advice supportive of the unique beauty present in Christian sisters regardless of their shape, size, or complexion.

A) My sister, go for the "well-kept" look. This includes things such as grooming one's hair (which is your glory – I Corinthians 11:15) and, oral hygiene (white teeth can only improve one's smile). And, whatever your wardrobe budget, strive to keep your clothes in good repair; it's not old-fashioned to be handy with a needle and thread (it may even save you paying the cleaners to do repairs). I have seen models who look as if they have slept a month in their clothes. I have even seen people who have paid large sums of money for clothes that have been deliberately torn and patched so as to make them look old and ragged. I must say that the shabby look is not necessarily sinful. However, I believe this style is one of those ridiculous fads that is not generally appealing to mature-minded people.

Additionally, a "well-kept" appearance serves to communicate that "I care about/respect myself." And, a mature brother wants a sister who cares for herself, as the Bible tells a man that he should love and cherish his wife as his own body (Ephesians 5:28 and 29).

B) Regardless of a sister's age, it is best to be in the best health one can be in, as this will cause one to look more attractive, feel better and live longer. There are many good books out now that deal with the concept of improving one's health (via foods eaten, sleep habits, exercise, etc.). Even the Apostle Paul said "For physical training is of some value…" (I Timothy 4:8a, *New International Version*).

C). Next, a mature brother is looking for a sister that is modest in her appearance (see I Timothy 2:9):

> Let me tell you a parable: A man walks into a small 24-hour grocery store at midnight. It's the middle of summer and the temperature is 90 degrees, even at midnight. When the man walks into the store, he is wearing a black ski-mask, a long black trench coat and is holding a large gun in his right hand. The only other customer in the store sees the man and begins screaming hysterically. When the man turns toward the screaming customer, a stock clerk slips up behind the man and knocks him over the head with a cast- iron, 12 inch frying pan. After the police arrive and the man regains consciousness, it becomes clear that the gun is only a toy gun and that the man was not intending to rob the store, but to purchase milk and cookies for a late-night snack.

People can act and even dress in a manner that evokes unintended responses. It is a common thing in today's time for some church ladies to dress in an indecent manner. When told that they are culpable in enticing men to lust, these women say "those men just have a dirty mind." Yes, those men may have a dirty mind, but what wisdom is there in lighting a match and throwing gasoline on the fire. As the man's appearance in the parable above was at least partly to blame for enticing the sin of violence (the frying pan blow), an improperly clad woman can entice brothers to the sin of lust.

Back to our original topic: a mature brother is distrustful of a woman with a skirt so short and tight that it looks like a diaper, or a long dress with a split as high as the moon (figuratively speaking), or cut so low at the top that you can see Christmas and New Years (figuratively speaking). A mature brother sees this type of sister and cannot help but wonder if her motives are pure. Even if a sister's motives are pure, her appearance may speak a different message. People say clothes don't matter, but God says to avoid the very appearance of evil (I Thessalonians 5:22). Having worked in law enforcement, I can say for a fact that Ladies of the Night reveal much of their body in order to seduce customers. When Christians take on this appearance (whether guilty of solicitation, or not), it is an association with an evil image. Christians can be fashionable without revealing that which should only be seen between an individual and his or her spouse.

While we're discussing modesty, let me say that Fire-Engine red shiny lips and Navy-Blue eyelids do not portray Biblical modesty. "Where are all the good men?" maybe they're in hiding from all these brazen, scary-looking church ladies.

D) A mature Christian brother wants someone who is feminine. We know that God frowns on the homosexual lifestyle (Romans 1:26 and 27). However, a more subtle tactic Satan uses in the church is to gradually edge people in the direction of believing that it is okay for a woman to look like a man (and, a man to look like a woman). Have you seen those church people who you cannot tell from their back if they are a man or a woman (see I Corinthians 6:9)? A mature Christian brother wants a sister who looks like a lady on all four sides, top and bottom.

As we move away from discussing appearance, let me share a scripture passage with those who say "Salvation is only in your heart and it does not matter what you do." The scripture is

James 2:17-26:

> 17 Even so faith, if it hath not works, is dead, being alone.
>
> 18 Yea, a man may say, Thou hast faith, and I have works: shew me thy faith without thy works, and I will shew thee my faith by my works.
>
> 19 Thou believest that there is one God; thou doest well: the devils also believe, and tremble.
>
> 20 But wilt thou know, O vain man, that faith without works is dead?
>
> 21 Was not Abraham our father justified by works, when he had offered Isaac his son upon the altar?
>
> 22 Seest thou how faith wrought with his works, and by works was faith made perfect?
> 23 And the scripture was fulfilled which saith, Abraham believed God, and it was imputed unto him for righteousness: and he was called the Friend of God.
>
> 24 Ye see then how that by works a man is justified, and not by faith only.
>
> 25 Likewise also was not Rahab the harlot justified by works, when she had received the messengers, and had sent them out another way?
>
> 26 For as the body without the spirit is dead, so faith without works is dead also.

II. GOODNESS. A mature brother is looking for a sister who is full of goodness. I have known people who have been church members, but were not so full of goodness. These persons were full of gossip and being around them was a burden.

A mature brother does not want to be involved with someone who will continually be wasting energy in spreading the latest scandal, as it is a distraction from God's work. That sister who is continually thinking on good things (Philippians 4:8) is a pleasure to be around and to talk to. With this type of person, you can depend on what they say to be true. A brother can trust this type of sister.

Another of the goodness attributes a brother is looking for in a sister is "selflessness" (not selfishness). See the parable of the Good Samaritan (Luke 10:25-37). Have you ever seen church ladies who manipulate and pressure their dates to buy them expensive gifts, not considering what their date can actually afford? You have some ladies who take a challenge in seeing just how much they can get a poor brother to spend. I have seen sisters so full of selflessness that they would willingly cook dinner for a struggling brother, let us say some brother who is a college student struggling to live within the budget of his scholarship and grant money. This type of sister does not have to have the immediate gratification of fancy dinners, because she knows if she marries a godly man and helps him through college, there will most likely be great opportunity later for fancy dinners.

III. GENTLENESS. When I was a child, there used to be a sister that loved to hug all the children. However, the lady was so loud, garish, and hugged the kids so roughly, that the kids were actually scared of her and would try to avoid her. This dear lady needed more gentleness. There may be some men who don't want a gentle wife. But, most men want a gentle wife. Gentleness in a woman does not mean she is less intelligent or that she is not outgoing. What it does mean is that she knows how to apply that right level of softness/ smoothness in how she approaches a situation. I have seen a sister who literally barks orders at her husband as if he were an oarsman on a roman slave ship. And, I have seen a lady assist her husband in wrestling/tying up a wild alligator (this is not a joke). Despite these exceptions, most mature brothers don't want to marry someone like their army buddy; they want someone gentle.

This concludes part one of the answer. However, we will continue this discussion later.

Part 2

I have considered for a long while what should be included in part two of this exposition. There is so much that could be said that I feel tempted in this next and final (?) edition to share general concepts (that are Biblically supported), which will directly (or indirectly) draw attention to additional, needful characteristics that a sister should exemplify in order to be the wife that a mature Christian brother wants/needs.

IV. HIERARCHY One of the serious shortcomings I see today among people who profess Christianity has to do with the need of sisters to understand the Biblical model of the "headship of the husband" in marriage. Sister, if you're already feeling greatly agitated in your mind simply due to my mention of the "headship of the husband", then you may be evidence of the growing tide of church women who reject this Biblical doctrine. Let me begin the discussion of the "headship of the husband" by saying a mature brother desires a Christian lady who not only thoroughly understands this concept, but is 100 percent committed to supporting her husband as the head by her actions. Before you eject to another web site, let's look at the Bible:

I Corinthians 11:3: "But I would have you know, that the head of every man is Christ; and the head of the woman is the man; and the head of Christ is God."

Let me quickly address two things a sister must understand – a wife who follows the Bible by acknowledging the headship of her husband is definitely not making some sort of declaration that she is of minimal value; and, this godly wife is not saying that her role in God's realm is unimportant. Notice, in the last part of the verse above, the fact that Christ has a head. Does this verse thereby discredit the mediatory function of Christ? Of course not! Christ having a head is not an insult, but addresses the hierarchy between Christ and God. So, a Christ-like wife is not insulted when someone reads I Corinthians 11:3.

Let's look at another scripture passage (Ephesians 5:22-25):

> 22 Wives, submit yourselves unto your own husbands, as unto the Lord.

> 23 For the husband is the head of the wife, even as Christ is the head of the church: and he is the saviour of the body.
> 24 Therefore as the church is subject unto Christ, so let the wives be to their own husbands in every thing.

> 25 Husbands, love your wives, even as Christ also loved the church, and gave himself for it;

Some have tried to nullify these verses by quoting verse 21, which gives a general instruction to all believers to submit to one another. However, attempting to use verse 21 to nullify the headship of the man is like saying John the Baptist was greater in authority than Jesus, because Jesus submitted to being baptized by John.

In a variety of things, a man may yield to what his wife desires (and wisely he should); however, this does not take away the fact that the husband is the highest human authority in the marital/family hierarchy. Hopefully, it is clear that when I say "husband," I am not talking about a live-in male lover; when the Bible says "husband," it is referring to a man who has legally committed himself in matrimony to ONE woman – a real husband is legally documented as such and is recognized by the local governing authorities as the husband.

Another trick I have seen used to nullify the headship of the husband is when people say there is no difference between men and women; the phrase "neither male nor female" of Galatians 3:28 is often misinterpreted. Galatians 3:28 could not possibly mean we should break down all differences between men and women (i.e., remove "MEN" and "WOMEN" signs which designate which church restrooms should be used by which gender).

Many years ago, I once had to utilize the restroom in what was a co-ed college dormitory. To my surprise, as I was in the restroom, in walked a young female student to utilize the facilities; I was not a Christian at the time, but I still did not believe this "neither male nor female" perverted doctrine when it came to sharing the same restroom at the same time.

What Galatians 3:28 addresses is the fact that through faith in Christ, all enter into the same union/unity known as the Body of Christ; there is no preference given to Jews over Gentiles, no preference even to free persons over those who may be locked in slavery, there is no circumcision given only to males (as in the Old Testament to identify with the Promise made by God to the Jews) – every person, regardless of race, nationality, even age, is free to come to Christ and become part of his body and become a fellow sibling to every other Christian.

However, this wonderful union of all believers does not mean my Christian niece who is around 12 years old will have the same role, or level of authority within the church as the aged women (see Titus 2:4). And, neither does Galatians nullify the headship of the man.

Let me also make the observation that the scripture passage above is not an endorsement that a husband can ask his wife to do something illegal, or immoral, or risky (such as running around outside carrying a metal rod during a lightning storm). A wife can and must refuse to take part in such dangerous activities.

The Biblical model that the husband is the head of the wife is not negated or voided when the husband is not as intelligent/smart as the wife. My admonition to all you brilliant ladies is not to marry until you find a man that you not only love, but respect enough to commit to as your head for as long as you both shall live, amen.

This is not to say that the wife is restricted from voicing her opinions. However, even when vigorously discussing opinions, the wife should do it in a way that attempts to show respect to her husband as the leader. Sisters, I know some of these brothers can come up with some wacky ideas. But, try to imagine that your husband is the president and that you are the vice-president – you wouldn't necessarily walk into the executive office and tell the president that his new tax cut will not work and that you refuse as the vice-president to allow him to implement the tax cut.

A wise vice-president would approach it by first pointing out the merits of the plan (if there are any) and then possibly outline some of the issues that appear to be detrimental to the success of the tax cut. A wise woman will try communicating in a similar wise way with her own husband.

Regardless of how much more spiritual a wife is than her husband, the husband is still Biblically the head. Again, the wife won't commit some sinful act because she is asked to do so by her husband. Ladies, before entering into matrimony with a man, it is so important to know what type of leader he is. A husband, in a Christian marriage, is not like a new puppy; you cannot return him (the husband) just because you find after taking him home that he (the husband) cannot be trained to fetch, sit or heel.

Let me say somewhat concerning this movement afoot where women are saying they are the head of their husbands – many don't make this statement explicitly, but they say things similar to one church lady, who remarked: "MY HUSBAND MAY WEAR THE PANTS, BUT I TELL HIM WHAT PAIR TO PUT ON!" [For those in various countries, "Wearing the Pants" is an expression used to designate the person that is the leader in a male-female relationship.] Other ladies subscribe to the concept that "My husband is the head and I am the neck, and the head does not turn left or right unless the neck turns the head." This type of belief system demonstrates a lady who is drastically out of step with the Biblical concept of the headship of the husband.

To further abuse and molest the Biblical concept of the headship of the husband, you have some church ladies who proclaim themselves to be their husband's Pastor (or even his bishop) – believe me, I am not making this up. These women disregard, or even misuse scriptures to justify why they do not have to follow the Bible (see ITimothy 3:1-7 regarding the qualifications of a Presiding Elder, or Pastor – called "Bishop" in the King James Version). Yes, I know you have some single women who have chosen to Pastor – but, I'd like to be a fly on the wall to see what happens when such a Bishop-woman marries a man who believes the Bible which authorizes him to be the head. I guess these Bishop women must take a vow not to marry, as is taught for all Pastors in certain cult churches (see ITimothy 4:1-3). I neither have the skill nor the cunning to reconcile the Bible with the concept of my wife trying to Pastor me; but, then I guess the purpose of Bible study is to rightly divide the Word of Truth, not to twist scripture interpretation to fit people's fleshly ambitions.

I was made aware of a case where a man believed he was called to Pastor in one area. However, his wife believed she was called to go somewhere else and Pastor. From what I understand, both decided to go their own way and each be a Pastor in different areas, quite some distance apart. I think this incidence shows why God did not say man and woman were 50% - 50% partners: each must give 100% fulfilling their unique Biblical role to the best of their ability.

Another case I am aware of involved a church lady who had not been married long. This dear lady spent significant amounts of time away from home running "revivals" from state to state to the point that her very young child began to exhibit signs of emotional stress.

Let's imagine a scenario where the wife is the Pastor and the husband is a lay member of her church. Let's imagine the husband says to the wife that he wants her to greatly decrease the amount of time that she is spending far away from home while their child is very young. Let's imagine the wife believes that everything she is doing in traveling so much is vitally necessary. And, invoking her Pastoral authority, she is unwilling to decrease her travel in spreading the gospel (she feels that she has an apostolic commission like the Apostle Paul). Who is the highest authority in this situation, the husband/head or his Pastor/Apostle wife?

Understand that this is only one of multiple issues you run into when we violate the Word of God regarding the role of the man and the woman.

One of the companies that I worked for converted to what you might call leaderless teams in one of its divisions. Throughout most of the division, the team managers were either moved to a new group or had their authority reduced to that of all other team members. As you can imagine, this resulted in great confusion and lack of productivity. In many teams, decisions that needed to be made, could not be made quickly as there was no member with the official title of team-manager who could make a decision when the team was incapable of agreeing on a plan of action. In like manner, you will have disagreements in marriage; and, if you are not clear on your Biblical roles, you are going to have some pretty intense communications late in the midnight hour, trying to establish a leader in the marriage.

But, enough of this particular thought. Let us move on.

I Peter 3:1-2 says:

> Likewise, ye wives, be in subjection to your own husbands; that, if any obey not the word, they also may without the word be won by the conversation of the wives; While they behold your chaste conversation coupled with fear.

These verses demonstrate how giving honor to your husband as the head of your home can even be used to draw him to obedience to God's Word – as the husband sees the wife's diligence to not just spouting Christian phrases, but living the parts of the Bible that are even sometimes challenging to obey.

You may ask: "Well, just how would a sister live out this giving of honor to her husband as the head, given that a mature Christian lady comes to marriage with her own unique personality, independence, and set of skills that make her an extremely valuable and important person in her own community, regardless of whether she marries or not?" Rather than try to describe every conceivable specific situation in which a wife must honor a husband, I would like to speak in a parabolic or allegorical fashion in describing a frame of mind a sister can have that will enable her to be what a mature brother needs.

V. VIRTUOUS WOMAN. First of all, ladies, you can look at courtship as being similar to an Executive Search. Let me explain what I mean by way of parable:

> In this parable we have a person who has a vision or plan to start a company. This person will be the president and Chief

Executive Officer (CEO) of this new company.

When I discuss the CEO below, I am really making reference to the Christian brother who is commissioned by God to be the Chief Executive (head) of the home. And, the company the CEO in our parable is starting represents the marriage/home that the Christian brother wishes to establish.

> The company president of our parable realizes he is not capable of launching this company alone and decides that he needs help, which includes one senior vice-president who has some qualities similar to those he has already and also potentially, greater strength in certain skills the president may not be as strong in.

Of course, this executive (vice-president) that the CEO is searching for represents the Christian woman. Ladies, let me make an observation right here: if the brother you are interested in is jealous of (threatened by) a woman because she is better than him in certain areas (e.g., financial planning), please re-consider whether you're willing and able to endure a lifetime commitment to a husband who is likely to inhibit you from exercising your unique abilities because of his jealousy and feelings of inadequacy. Remember: the husband being the leader does not mean he is more skilled than his wife in every area.

Back to our parable:
> Some of the specific skill sets that the president in our parable is searching for will depend on the vision/plan he has for his company and the nature of what the company produces. Similarly, some of the characteristics the Christian brother is looking for will depend on his vision/plans. For example, a brother who has a vision of spending his life running a vacation ranch for troubled teens high in the mountains will possibly need a wife who is capable of living in a rural

setting, or at least willing to learn the things necessary for living in a rural area (e.g., how to administer certain types of first aid for dangers/injuries more prevalent on a mountainous ranch). The advice I will give to you sisters is to learn much about the brother you are interested in as a prospective husband. His physical good looks are important, but some women marry without learning about who the brother is on the inside. Shame on you, if you married a brother without finding out that he has a lifelong plan of building his own boat so that he can sail to the Antarctic to study the feeding habits of penguins.

As you may have surmised, two people who are Christians and find each other physically attractive (who may even be good friends) may still be an awful match as a married couple.

In our parable, our CEO will have objectives of what the company is to achieve. A vice-president (VP) who is of any use, is a VP who believes in and supports the CEO's overall plans to reach those objectives. Dear ladies, don't take that VP position if you don't have a clue as to what the CEO's objectives are, or his plan for achieving them.

If the CEO has no objectives, no plans, no direction, no priorities in life – well, why would you choose a VP position under a CEO who is wandering around aimlessly like a lost child?

In many cases, a good CEO will delegate responsibility to the VP for defining the strategy for achieving a pre-established objective. Allow me to provide more clarification: As a husband, it is my desire that my family have good medical care. After years of participation in a particular medical plan, I found I was greatly displeased with the level of service. As my wife worked in the medical field, I handed (delegated) the decision to her to determine the best medical plan available.

She also chose our doctors within the plan. As the head, I had an established goal of providing good medical coverage for my family. Given my wife's special expertise in the medical field, I completely turned the analysis and decision over to her as to which plan we should select.

After completing the analysis, my wife presented her decision to me with the reasoning behind it and we implemented her choice.

A. Industriousness. One of the traits that I am sure a CEO is looking for in a VP is that of a willingness to work hard.

Similarly, the book of Proverbs identifies a virtuous woman (good wife) as an industrious woman. Proverbs 31:13 "She seeketh wool, and flax, and worketh willingly with her hands."
This is true whether a woman works in an office building or is a Stay-At-Home mom. (In my opinion, the woman who successfully cares for a home and family is just as worthy of honor, praise and respect as the person who manages a successful business)

Show me a wife who avoids all work, and I'd almost guarantee that I can show you an unhappy husband.

A woman afraid of work, should possibly consider not getting married until she has resolved this fear.

One of the disadvantages of a wife who avoids all work is that she will easily drive a working-class man into poverty. She will buy new clothes when those she has only need a little needle and thread to repair; she will spend hours chattering on the phone rather than using letter writing for some of her communication to friends far away; she will buy groceries based on convenience alone (spending her scarce few grocery dollars on a teeny-tiny box of rice that cooks in one minute as opposed to a 50-pound bag of rice that must be cooked longer but costs almost the same as the tiny box of rice).

What is so interesting to me is why people with money problems shop so inefficiently (buying pre-processed and pre-cooked items that are much more expensive).

I guess what I am talking about here used to be called "Mother-wit".

B. Nurturing. Speaking of work in the home, one of the tasks that fall to a large percentage of ladies is the preparation of nourishment for their entire households.

While some belittle this task, Proverbs 31:15 praises the woman who does this well ("She riseth also while it is yet night, and giveth meat to her household...") Let me tell you that the virtuous woman does not feed her family unhealthy food because it is inconvenient and time consuming to provide wholesome food. I know some of you may not like what I am about to say, but too many mothers throughout the industrialized world waste money buying junk food to feed to their family at breakfast; any time you have over-processed bleached grain products that have been saturated in sugary sweeteners, pouring a cup of milk over this concoction in no way provides a complete nutritious breakfast (despite what some breakfast cereal companies say). Do I need to say that a donut-pastry and a cola soft-drink is also not a wholesome lunch. Instead of spending so much time designing a wedding dress, spend some of your time learning what the basic food groups are.

No! the Four basic food groups are not: "Drive-through, Home-delivery, TV Dinners and Pizza".

When the pizza delivery man knows your whole family by first name (even grandpa), you may have an instance of a nurturer who is not nurturing.

When your children have the full set of drive-through burger-shack toys for all four seasons of the year, you may have an instance of a nurturer who is not nurturing. Let me say ladies, that every adult should try to learn the basics of what is proper nutrition.

Nutrition is such an important thing, that I believe those of us who are more blessed should help the impoverished.

However, In many cases, lack of nutrition occurs in homes where there is enough money to buy the essentials; the lack of proper nutrition in these cases may be due to lack of knowledge.

C. Organized. The latter part of Proverbs 31:15 ("and a portion to her maidens") shows us that the virtuous woman is an organizer.

If, as a single woman, you have a reputation for being disorganized, you will not make a good VP for the CEO (your husband).

It is amazing to me how intelligent adults in the work world are so disorganized that they do not live by a budget. You have some who do not even know what I mean by a budget (financially speaking). If you are always late for work, for dates, for church, for school, how will you be successful as a VP to your husband.

The virtuous woman, in scripture, not only organizes her own time but manages her maidens (her workers). But you say that you do not have a staff. Well, if you have children (or will ever have children in the future) you have (or will have) staff.

What perplexes me is women who complain of having to do all the washing, cooking, cleaning, etc., and they have perfectly healthy children living in the home who are tall enough to reach the sink where the dirty dishes are, and smart enough to assemble video games and attach them to the TV, but they're incapable of using the clothes washer and dryer.

The virtuous woman sees the resources at her disposal and makes use of them. If you hear what I am saying, you might be able to reduce the amount of money you are spending on maid services.

D. Shrewd/Business-like/Professional. The virtuous woman of Proverbs 31:16 has business skills. In the example cited in the verse, she is able to recognize a good real estate deal.

You may say that you don't need any business skills whatsoever, because your CEO (e.g., your husband) will have all the skills. Bad, Bad, Bad mistake: if the CEO becomes ill, or otherwise incapacitated, then one of the responsibilities of the VP is to take over and keep the company (or home in our case) from totally falling apart; remember that little phrase in the wedding vow: "in sickness and in health" – yes, your marriage really is supposed to survive through the serious illness of a spouse.

E. Generous. Proverbs 31:20 says of the virtuous woman: "She stretcheth out her hand to the poor; yea, she reacheth forth her hands to the needy." I live in one of the wealthiest countries in the world; why is it that so many church people are not even concerned about the poor around them, and in other countries around the world? This lack of concern may be a symptom of selfishness and greed. Like a farmer drives a team of mules, some wives drive their husbands to work one, two, and maybe even three jobs to acquire luxuries.

But, you show me a woman who is generous to the poor, and I probably can show you the wife who will place the health and welfare of her husband above trying to acquire luxuries through nagging him to work around the clock. Before you buy those five pairs of shoes, I ask you to consider buying four pair and dedicating the price of the fifth pair to the work of God.

If you desire, I can refer you to at least two organizations doing a great work who need funds – one of which feeds and educates poor children.

F. Honor the CEO (husband) of your home above all others. If you were placed in charge of a renovation at a manufacturing plant, would you be more concerned about the specifications the CEO of the company wanted you to adhere to, or would you be more concerned about the specifications your mama wanted you to adhere to? You might think it is obvious that the CEO's wishes should carry more weight; however, consider the myriad of cases where friends and relatives opinions are considered more important than the husbands concerning matters relating to the married couple's household.

Again, I am not saying the husband is always correct; but his wishes should be at least more carefully considered in matters related to the couple's household, even if the couple decides to take the advice (not demands) of friends or relatives. I hope it is obvious here that we are not speaking about a husband asking his wife to do something illegal, immoral or dangerous.

Let me give you at least one parable on the subject of honoring:

> We have Uncle Butterbean who lives across town but comes to visit a young couple on occasion. Whenever Uncle Butterbean comes over, he goes out on the patio after dinner and takes a nap in a lounge chair. The wife in this young couple truly loves and respects her Uncle Butterbean; whenever Uncle Butterbean is napping, his niece (the wife) is ever so careful not to let the kids play ping pong on the patio, and careful not to let the dog out on the patio, in order to keep from disturbing Uncle Butterbean. The wife, who has her workout bicycle on the patio, even changes her exercise schedule when Uncle Butterbean is napping so as not to disturb him.

However, any sunny Saturday afternoon that the young wife's husband happens to be napping in his hammock on the patio, the kids are allowed to play ping pong, the dog can run around barking, and the wife will get most indignant if asked to exercise later. The kids are even allowed to have water fights (throwing water-balloons and buckets of water back and forth across the patio at each other).

Now I ask you, what non-verbal message is the wife giving her husband – It appears to me that Uncle Butterbean is honored much more in that home by the wife than the husband and leader of that house.

G. Desires her husband. Years ago, as I sat in a church youth program, I heard a very young man proclaim that sex was spiritual and was not to be enjoyed.

Apparently, he was not familiar with scripture passages such as those found in the Song of Solomon or in Proverbs 5:15-21. Yes, there is a holy and spiritual aspect of sex, but God indeed made this conjugal privilege to be enjoyed within the bounds of marriage.

Hebrews 13:4 says "Marriage is honourable in all, and the bed undefiled: but whoremongers and adulterers God will judge."

Let me make a very important observation before I get to my main point; the great majority of Christian men really look forward to this great conjugal privilege. So, to make my main point, the great majority of Christian men are desirous of a wife who (within the bounds of marriage) will be passionately desirous of enjoying her husband, as relates to this conjugal privilege.

If you feel that it is your mission to make the marriage bedroom as cold as the South Pole (metaphorically speaking), then I can almost assure you that your husband will have major, major, major regrets about his matrimonial decision.

Let me also raise a problem that I hope you will never, never, never be guilty of:

> Be very careful never ever to give the impression to your husband that you are using the bedroom as a ploy to take over the headship of the family. I have heard how some wives are only willing to have pleasure in conjugal privileges with their husbands if his preaching and teaching meets with her approval; or, only if the husband is willing to buy that $500 dress; or, only when he has completed a list of chores the wife has assigned to him (e.g., wash the dog, scrub the kitchen floor, shampoo the carpet) – the danger in this is that you reduce the conjugal privilege to a commerce/business transaction (which, if you were not married, would be a jail-able offense).

I Corinthians 7:5 says "Defraud ye not one the other, except it be with consent for a time, that ye may give yourselves to fasting and prayer; and come together again, that Satan tempt you not for your incontinency." Despite what you may have learned at the last lady's get-together, when a man and woman get married, you no longer belong just to yourselves.

Just back up one verse to I Corinthians 7:4: "The wife hath not power of her own body, but the husband: and likewise also the husband hath not power of his own body, but the wife." Yes, everything must be done properly, with appropriate sensitivity (of course a spouse incapacitated by a severe illness may be limited in participating in the conjugal privilege).

Yet, don't become like the wife whose husband wrote a book about the 365 excuses per year that his wife had for not enjoying the conjugal privilege with him. When you take on the attitude of this wife, you play right into the plan of Satan. I Corinthians 7:2 says "Nevertheless, to avoid fornication, let every man have his own wife, and let every woman have her own husband."

Marriage is a challenge and requires lots of hard work. Marriage is not for everyone, as Jesus confirms for us in Matthew 19:11-12. There are advantages to staying unmarried.

My advice is that you not marry unless you personally want to be married (not that you were coerced into marriage), and that you are willing to strive to be the model wife as defined by the Bible.

Don't be like this one man who gave me an overly critical evaluation of the construction work another saint had done. Apparently, the overly critical individual had some expertise in the area of carpentry; however, the home that this critical individual's wife and children were residing in appeared to leave much (very much) to be desired. Don't be like this man: full of knowledge, but with no application.

Let me end on this word:

If you are a faithful servant of God, you are a sister of priceless value; do not settle for just any man as your husband. Be the best and expect the best, and don't settle for anything less because you deserve God's very BEST!

As my mother taught me: *if you are single, you can always get married, but if you get married, then you cannot simply get unmarried.*